PIERRE F. WALTER

THE RESTRICTION

OF NATIONAL SOVEREIGNTY

From the Early Peace Plans to a World Government

Non est potestas Super Terram quæ Comparetur ei Iob. 41. 24.

LEVIATHAN

Or

THE MATTER, FORME and POWER of A COMMON-WEALTH ECCLESIASTICALL and CIVIL.

By THOMAS HOBBES of MALMESBVRY.

Published by Sirius-C Media Galaxy LLC

http://sirius-c-publishing.com

http://siriuscmedia.com

http://ipublica.com

ISBN 978-1-453718-07-0

Contact Information Pierre F. Walter

publisher@sirius-c-publishing.com

About Pierre F. Walter

http://drpfw.info

Quotation Suggestion

Pierre F. Walter, *The Restriction of National Sovereignty: From the Early Peace Plans to a World Government*, Newark: Sirius-C Media Galaxy LLC, 2010

About the Author

Pierre F. Walter is an author, international lawyer, researcher, corporate trainer, and lecturer. After finalizing studies in German Law, International Law and *European integration* with diplomas obtained in 1981 through  1983, he graduated in December 1987 at the Law Faculty of the University of Geneva as *Docteur en Droit* in international law.

The doctorate was funded by scholarships from the *Swiss Institute of Comparative Law*, Lausanne, and from the *University of Geneva*, as well as a Fulbright Travel Grant for an assistantship with Professor Louis B. Sohn at *UGA Law School Department of International Law*, Athens, Georgia, USA, in 1985. Pierre F. Walter also served as a research assistant to *Freshfields, Bruckhaus, Deringer*, Cologne, Germany in 1983 and to *Lalive Lawyers*, Geneva, in 1987.

Pierre F. Walter writes and lectures in English, German and French languages; he has written *more than ten thousand pages* embracing all literary genres, including *novels, short stories, film scripts, essays, selfhelp books, monographs* and extended *book reviews*. Also a pianist and composer, he has realized 40 CDs with *jazz, newage* and *relaxation music*.

Pierre F. Walter's professional publications span the domains *International Law, Criminal Law, Holistic Science, Psychology, Education, Shamanism, Ecology, Spirituality, Quantum Physics, Systems Theory, Natural Healing, Peace Research, Personal Growth, Selfhelp* and *Consciousness Research*. 110 Book Reviews, thirty-eight audio books and more than hundred video lectures were realized in the years 2005-2010. Besides, Pierre F. Walter is author and editor of *Great Minds Series*, which features scientists, artists and authors of genius from Leonardo to Fritjof Capra.

Pierre F. Walter publishes via his Delaware firm *Sirius-C Media Galaxy LLC* and the imprints IPUBLICA and Sirius-C Media (SCM).

Dedicated to Barack Obama

CONTENTS

Published by Sirius-C Media Galaxy LLC, 2010

NOTES   226

Annotations

Nationalism, the patriotic spirit, class and race consciousness, are all ways of the self, and therefore separative. After all, what is a nation but a group of individuals living together for economic and self-protective reasons? Out of fear and acquisitive self-defense arises the idea of my country, with its boundaries and tariff walls, rendering brotherhood and the unity of man impossible.

– J. Krishnamurti, *Education and the Significance of Life (1978)*

There exists perhaps no conception the meaning of which is more controversial than that of sovereignty. It is an indisputable fact that this conception, from the moment when it was introduced into political science until the present day, has never had a meaning which was universally agreed upon.

– Lassa Oppenheim, *International Law (1928)*

INTRODUCTION

What is National Sovereignty?

What is Sovereignty?

Sovereignty is a concept that describes the *scope of power of rulers, sovereigns, heads of state or governments;* it came upon us from the Romans who expressed it as the idea that the Emperor exercised an absolute reign; the same idea reigned in old Egypt where the Pharaoh had absolute power over the land and the people.

The ancient peoples did not yet talk about *sovereignty* in the conceptual sense we know it, but the idea was basically the same. It has to be seen that the monarchs of the feudal aristocracy during the Middle-Ages were not sovereigns in that quality as their rulership was limited, and not absolute.

The feudal system however was rather the exception, while absolute sovereignty was later established as the rule in international law. There was nonetheless a continuity in the basic concept of sovereignty, while its scope and its possible limits were a matter of scholarly debate, from the time of the Romans through to the present day. This is how the concept changed in its definition, scope, and application, until a certain uniformity and consensus was reached during the *Age of Enlightenment.*

The current notion of state sovereignty was laid down in the *Treaty of Westphalia (1648)*, which marked the end of the *Thirty Years War (1618-1648)* and which, in relation to states, codified the *basic principles of territorial integrity, border inviolability, and supremacy of the state,* as opposed to the authority of the

Published by Sirius-C Media Galaxy LLC, 2010

Church. It was from that time also that international law described a sovereign is a supreme lawmaking authority.

After the centuries of the abusive regime of the Church, with all their witchhunts and the holocaust perpetrated by the Inquisition in Europe, sovereignty reemerged as a concept in the late 1500s, a time when civil wars had created a craving for stronger central authority, when monarchs had begun to gather power into their own hands at the expense of the nobility, and the modern nation state was emerging. Jean Bodin and Thomas Hobbes presented theories of sovereignty calling for strong central authority in the form of absolute monarchy.

In his treatise *On Sovereignty (1576/2009)*, Jean Bodin argued that it is inherent in the nature of the state that sovereignty is *absolute* and *perpetual*. This modern conceptualization of sovereignty later led to what is called *absolutism*, and what became the leading version of rulership for the French kings. In fact, the strange thing is that when the Church began to lose its absolute power in Europe, the sovereign power of the monarch was defined with religious overtones. Bodin and other scholars wrote that the doctrine of sovereignty is conferred by divine law; this is how the idea came up that kings enjoyed some form of *divine right*.

Thomas Hobbes, in his book *Leviathan (1651/2006)*, introduced an early version of the *social contract*, a theory later taken up and developed by Jean-Jacques Rousseau (1712-1778). Hobbes deduced from the definition of sovereignty that it must be *absolute* and *indivisible*. The idea that the ruler's sovereignty is in effect conferred to him by the people in return for his maintaining their safety, led him to conclude that if the ruler fails to do this, the people are released from their obligation to obey him, which can as a hypothesis be seen verified later on with the *French Revolution (1789-1799)*.

Niccolò Machiavelli, Thomas Hobbes, John Locke, and Montesquieu are key figures in the unfolding of the concept of sovereignty. The second book of Rousseau's *Social Contract (1762/1997)* deals with sovereignty and its rights.

Sovereignty, or the general will, is inalienable, for the will cannot be transmitted; it is indivisible, since it is essentially general; it is infallible and always right, determined and limited in its power by the common interest; it acts through laws.

In the third book, he argued that 'the growth of the state will give the trustees of public authority more and means to abuse their power', which is exactly what was going to be seen on the political arena later on. And here we can see one of the reasons why the French Revolution shifted the possession of sovereignty from the sovereign ruler to the nation and its people.

Published by Sirius-C Media Galaxy LLC, 2010

A Modern Definition

West's Encyclopedia of American Law (2008) defines sovereignty as 'the supreme, absolute, and uncontrollable power by which an independent state is governed and from which all specific political powers are derived; the intentional independence of a state, combined with the right and power of regulating its internal affairs without foreign interference'.

Sovereignty is the power of a state to do everything necessary to govern itself, such as making, executing, and applying laws, imposing and collecting taxes, making war and peace and forming treaties or engaging in commerce with foreign nations.

The individual states of the United States do not possess the powers of external sovereignty, such as the right to deport undesirable persons, but each does have certain attributes of internal sovereignty, such as the power to regulate the acquisition and transfer of property within its borders. The sovereignty of a state is determined with reference to the U.S. Constitution, which is 'the supreme law of the land.'

Overview

In *Chapter One*, entitled *The Rise of National Sovereignty*, I would like to sensibilize the reader to perceiving history and political change not just on a rationality scale, but as a matter of cyclic phases in human evolution.[1] This is not a new idea but a perennial insight that was part of the ancient science codex in which the science of astrology was considered a supreme tool for predicting change and evolution. Astrology has predicted the *Aquarius Age* to take its course from about 2000 to 2020; it is the successor of the *Pisces Age*. What does that mean? The Zodiac teaches us that life doesn't consist of single isolated events but that all is *interconnected and cyclic*, and therefore subject to repetition and spiraled nonlinear evolution. Astrologers always emphasized the high importance of cyclical thinking as opposed to linear thinking. In the evolution of humanity, there are various cycles that describe the characteristics of humanity's phylogenetic development.

These cycles are generally very long; they do not just embrace years, not just decades, but centuries and millennia. The most recent of these cycles, that we just left, the *Pisces Age*, lasted approximately two thousand years. The Pisces Age is associated with the 12th House of the Zodiac and thus with the collective, as opposed to the individual, with mass obsessions, and focus on illness instead of health, with secrecy and taboo instead of free speech, and segregation instead of integration. The Ruler of the 12th House is *Neptune* as the ruler of Pisces which symbolizes water and emotions in their raw,

Published by Sirius-C Media Galaxy LLC, 2010

non-integrated form. The Aquarius Age, by contrast, the era we are just about entering, is associated with the 11th House of the Zodiac and thus with universal love, friendship and brotherhood, with communication beyond borders, and sharing of ideas across cultural boundaries. It is ruled by *Uranus* and associated with the element *air* emphasizing communication as the single most important activity during this cycle.

Let us have a look now at the essential differences in the social and political paradigms that are associated with Pisces Age, on one hand, and Aquarius Age, on the other.

Pisces Age	Aquarius Age
linear, dogmatic, mechanistic thinking	cyclic, functional, systemic thinking
group over individual	power of the individual and groupings
uniformity, dogmatism, tyranny	diversity, democracy, shared power
fundamentalism, absolutism	functionalism
authority and hero worship	self-power
obedience to leaders	obedience to self
mass education, alphabetization	individualized education
mass media, mass manipulation	media on demand, media choices
lack of identity and spirituality	high identity, self-chosen spirituality
lack of autonomy for the young	high autonomy for the young
high cultural uniformity	high cultural diversity
co-dependence, narcissism	emotionally integrated sexuality
locality, provinciality	non-locality, globality, universality
macro-industry	micro-industry
environmental pollution	environmental consciousness
hierarchical and pyramidal structures	flat and neuronal structures
political opacity	political transparence
regional and national values	global values
discarding out, segregating	embracing, integrating

mind-body split	mind-body harmony
accumulation, agglomeration	diversification, recycling
minorities considered as nuisance	minorities considered as enrichment
habitual career choices valued	unusual career choices valued
the neurotic, compulsive character	the genital, flexible character

The general trend under the Aquarius Age will be away from collectivism and toward individualism, away from standard opinions and rules toward more freedom for setting and living our own personalized standards and ways of life.

The regard of the state upon the citizen will largely shift. While within the authoritarian if not totalitarian state of the Pisces Age, the citizen was a *subject or vassal*, for the democratic Aquarian state, the citizen is a *customer*.

The Aquarius Age shall provide the individual with a greater sphere of self-expression and more options for associating with peers and groupings that pursue similar goals, even if those goals largely differ from the opinions or the life style of the average individual, or the majority. There will be definitely more space and recognition for *alternative life styles*. The influence of social and political bodies over the individual will decrease and become more smooth.

Rulership will adopt more of a caretaking nature and a kind of creative partnership with the people under the rule. The leadership paradigm will change from leadership to *stewardship* or servant-leadership, as I have outlined it in my *Idiot Guide to Servant Leadership (2010)*.

In the Pisces Age we see tradition often as a way to justify repression or even tyranny; typically, tradition-holders and tradition-seekers are politically right wing and do all to sabo-

Published by Sirius-C Media Galaxy LLC, 2010

tage the upsurge of a truly pluralistic society. The Aquarian thinker is deeply concerned with *reforming and renewing* tradition. In Aquarian culture, tradition will be valued as a useful tool for acquiring insights about the human nature, without more. The Aquarius Age is likely to create a society that is highly complex and highly parceled but in which every individual has a much higher chance than before to make out a niche, a viable space and protection as well as social contact in interest circles of the most various kinds.

Chapter Two, entitled *The United States of Europe, Utopia or Future Reality?*, starts with a somewhat uncanny question. Will the process of *European Integration* lead Europe to being one day a second USA, or rather, USE? Or is that altogether a crazy idea?

While this may be a dream or a nightmare, depending on your personal opinion, are there any rational and political elements to be made out that could justify such a comparison? But anyway, such a comparison can only be the starting point of a reflection that focuses upon *giving peace to the whole of the globe.* The idea of a *world government* is very old; it was first voiced with European philosophers Kant and Rousseau, and others. But of course, the 'world', politically speaking, at that time was Europe, not the whole of the globe, as it is today.

At least until the *Declaration of Independence (1776),* Europe represented the world. In that sense, the European unification can be seen as a *model* and from that perspective, in turn, it makes sense to compare it with the establishment and unification of the United States of America.

Next, when we look at the details of the old peace plans, we see a basic idea; it's the insight that only through a *restriction of national sovereignty*, as a voluntary act by the nations who wish to unite their efforts for founding a world government, we can possibly achieve world peace. Of course, many doubt either the idea itself, or else the readiness of our nation states to be motivated for such a step *by a true wish for world peace*, rather than for gaining the ultimate superpower for an even tighter control of the citizen. If I may evaluate the positions, I can see that among younger people, many doubt the very idea while oder people and particularly those who have experienced a war or civil war are more open toward the idea but they may doubt the political readiness at present.

The next question, then, is if that unification should be achieved through integration or through enacting a constitution? The same question was being asked for European integration, and it has unfortunately divided Europeans into two camps, the *Integrationalists* and the *Constitutionalists*. However, in practice, the gradual process of step-by-step integration is what is daily reality in Europe, and was so since the foundation of the *European Coach and Steel Community (ECSC) in 1951*.

In **Chapter Three**, entitled *The Restriction of National Sovereignty*, I further outline the idea of limiting national sovereignty as a growing concern in international law from the moment governments entered the market place to behave like private traders. This subject, which was the focal point of my doctoral thesis back in 1987, is important enough for the United Nations' *International Law Commission (ILC)* to adopt an international convention, in 2004. Before the first precedent,

Published by Sirius-C Media Galaxy LLC, 2010

*The Schooner Exchange (1812)*², nation states indeed enjoyed an *unlimited national sovereignty* over their territory, and in addition, in their quality as sovereigns, also in front of the tribunals of other states. Why was from that point in time national sovereignty restricted under the so-called *restrictive immunity doctrine?*

To say it in plain English, it was because states began to rampantly abuse their sovereignty, and thus their power, by buying and selling goods, thus behaving like traders, but then, when it was to pay the bill, they claimed sovereign immunity, and the traders who had contracted with them, were engaging huge financial losses. These losses, one must imagine, are always in the millions of dollars, because when states behave on the international stage, they behave like *big* actors.

As a result, international scholars, lawyers, departments of state and courts began to change the reigning paradigm, and *restricted sovereign immunity* in a way that, when the activity in question was commercial, no immunity was to be granted to the foreign state. In that transitory period, until the doctrine was really established, the results could go either way, but often they went against the state claiming immunity, and governments were really thrown over the head, and had to pay. Sometimes it really went south, as the traders got a valid judgment but then couldn't execute it, as regarding the protection of foreign property, international law does not admit a restriction of sovereignty to the extent this is the case for jurisdictional immunities. So, in some spectacular cases, there was a bitter pill to choke at the end, but as most nations want to comply with international law, and if it's only to avoid being labeled as screwed and twisted, in most cases where there was a valid judgment and immunity was denied, states paid the bill, so that finally justice was being done to everybody involved. Now, I bring this argument here as a metaphor, for it has to be seen that the restriction of national sovereignty in matters of foreign sovereign immunity assumes a *signal function*, as it was a novelty event in international law and led to a real change of the paradigm.

What I am saying is that if it was possible to render more justice in international trading through a restricted immunity doctrine, by restricting national sovereignty, then this can be achieved also in other areas, on the political arena, for example. If international law generally admits that national sovereignty *can be restricted for reasons of lawful behavior and for equity reasons,* then the idea can be made fruitful for bringing about an even greater paradigm change in international law and practice, that is a restriction of national sovereignty *for preserving world peace.*

I am convinced that this will not happen without a triggering event or events, as power has a self-preserving function; but on the other hand I know that the day will come where the abusive character of national sovereignty will be so blatantly obvious, because major destruction and human loss will have to be complained, and down road humanity will see no better choice than to advance toward a paradigm of absolute restriction of national sovereignty for the single reason of preserving world peace. Then, a world government will see its day in court, and has a chance to be realized in no-time, while there will probably be *no time yet* for such a paradigm change to occur tomorrow or next year.

Published by Sirius-C Media Galaxy LLC, 2010

The **Bibliography** is shared for all my publications and contains all my research references.

From The Same Author is a complete bibliography of my nonfiction literary production, including my audio books and my video channels and podcasting episodes.

The **Monographs-Audio Synopsis** shows the relation between audio books and their published text, within all the fourteen monographs.

CHAPTER ONE

The Rise of National Sovereignty

The Necessity to Restrict National Sovereignty

The single most important leverage for world peace is the *restriction of national sovereignty* to a residual concept, transferring the ensuing sovereignty power vacuum to an *international organism* that shall be competent for matters of 'world government', as for example the peaceful settlement of conflicts, international currency management, ecological sanity requirements for businesses and related conflict solution, international arbitrage services, as well as strategic, economic or humanitarian help for developing countries, and last not least survival support for ethnic, racial or otherwise endangered minorities and tribal cultures wherever located, within any of the nation states.

With the transfer of national sovereignty to a supranational authority, the nation states party of such an international agreement, that forms the constitutional charta of the authority to be created, would transfer all competencies for handling the above-mentioned international affairs to that organism called 'World Government' or otherwise.

The idea is not new, as I will demonstrate below, where I report some of the well-known *Plans for Eternal Peace in Europe*, as they were brought up by great philosophers such as Immanuel Kant, Jean-Jacques Rousseau, and others.

Interestingly enough, from the many thinkable solutions for establishing world peace, these plans all converged to a single monolithic idea, which is the *restriction of national sovereignty*; it is interesting because when the first of these ideas emerged, in the 17th century, the nation state itself was still in the cradle; it was around that time that the very notion of the nation state was beginning to emerge in international law.

Before that time, the 'state' was notably not yet a political and legal entity as in the craftsmen-society, a concept of 'national power' was not yet existent; power structures at that time were by and large *regional*, and it was through inbreeding, that is the fusion of large nobility blood lines, that this regional power structure gradually expanded into the later nation states. But with that to happen, there was at the same time an inherent danger to the peace of that ancient society; the danger was that the cross-breeding structure within the European nobility that was *actually interlinking the old world*, was breaking apart because of the artificial construct of 'national sovereignty'.

Thus, as most international law scholars agree, with the abandonment of that kind of flexible 'networked' nobility structure of the princedoms and kingdoms developing into a rigid scheme of nations who, through the very idea of national sovereignty, were fundamentally hostile to each other, the soil for all wars and civil wars to occur later in history was prepared. It is national sovereignty, as an idea, which by the way is not something rooted in history, but a construct that was prepared in most of its contours by *Count Niccolò Machiavelli*, that was the single most explosive political concept in human history, leading to rampant political violence and tyranny, and endless wars and civil wars culminating in the two World Wars, in the 20th century.

Published by Sirius-C Media Galaxy LLC, 2010

What I am saying here is not an insight that can only be gained now, in the 21st century, but a fact that already some brilliant contemporaries of Machiavelli identified, which is why they were alarmed about 'the state of the world' and came up with peace plans, some of which were denominated as 'urgency solutions'.

Alvin Toffler writes in his book *The Third Wave (1984)*, in a chapter entitled 'A Frenzy of Nations':

Alvin Toffler

Starting with the American and French revolutions and continuing through the nineteenth century, a *frenzy of nationalism* swept across the industrializing parts of the world. Germany's three hundred and fifty petty, diverse, quarreling mini-states needed to be combined into a single national market – das Vaterland. Italy – broken into pieces and ruled variously by the House of Savoy, the Vatican, the Austrian Habsburgs, and the Spanish Bourbons – had to be united. Hungarians, Serbs, Croats, Frenchmen, and others all suddenly developed mystical affinities for their fellows. Poets exalted the national spirit. Historians discovered long-lost heroes, literature, and folklore. Composers wrote hymns to nationhood. *All at precisely the moment when industrialization made it necessary.*[3]

I found Toffler's books only after finalizing this study, and to my surprise I note a similar line of reasoning. In my study *Natural Order (2010),* I am discussing the entire human evolution as a process that went over three basic phases, *thesis, antithesis* and *synthesis*. And with Toffler I find the same kind of reasoning expressed as a concept of *three waves,* the *First Wave,* which I called thesis or original order, the *Second Wave,* which

I call antithesis or the disturbed or industrial order and the *Third Wave*, synthesis, which could be called the new order.

Toffler pursues on the subject of nationalism:

Alvin Toffler

What one saw, therefore, in one country after another, was the rise of this powerful new entity – the nation. In this way the world map came to be divided into a set of neat, nonoverlapping patches of red, pink, orange, yellow, or green, *and the nation-state system became one of the key structures of Second Wave civilization.*[4]

The following quote stands symbolic for the injustice and immense cruelty and power of the antithesis over the natural order, and explains in a metaphorical manner the chaos it created in the world to this very day:

Alvin Toffler

In reality, negotiations between *Second Wave* merchants and *First Wave* people over sugar, copper, cocoa, or other resources were often totally lopsided.

On one side of the table sat money-shrewd European or American traders backed by huge companies, extensive banking networks, powerful technologies, and strong national governments. On the other one might find a local lord or tribal chieftain whose people had scarcely entered the money system and whose economy was based on small-scale agriculture or village crafts. On one side sat the agents of a thrusting, alien, mechanically advanced civilization, convinced of its own superiority and ready to use bayonets or machine guns to prove it. On the other sat representatives of small prenational tribes or principalities, armed with arrows and spears.[5]

Published by Sirius-C Media Galaxy LLC, 2010

Sovereignty Going Global?

We are today in a completely different world. While we still have national governments, national identities and national budgets, and while we still have borders and passport controls, the world has considerably changed since the 17th century. It's virtually no more the same world. We are all interconnected today through not only the electronic wires, the Internet, and wireless communication, handphones, and satellites, and worldwide publicity, but we are also having the knowledge now, through quantum physics and other cutting-edge sciences that we are *not alone and separate* as human being, but interlinked through the quantum field, the underlying matrix of all life in the universe.

Today, the worldwide structural shifts in the economies, and the gradual formation of what could be called a global network economy forces people to change their business and their personal paradigms. It forces them to look at life in an entirely different way.

These global structural changes already now, but more still in the decades to come, will force many traditional businesses to renew themselves in a way to being more flexible, more 'movable' and more unconventional for implementing new and integrated solutions. Economies are likely to crash if they are unable to do the structural changes that globalization requires. New ways for financing projects of global dimensions will be found. Today, not only economists begin to doubt if the world economy is going to be maintained on the sole basis of a paper currency such as the dollar; there will probably be a pool of prime currencies that compose, and safeguard, the 'world currency' of the future. This process of working out something like a 'world currency pool' is likely to take a *leveraging function* in the paradigm change from sovereign nations to a world government where every nation joins in with all their cultural, ethnic and social diversity, but with a shared restricted sovereignty that would relegate world wars to the past.

The concept of sovereignty, today, cannot be seen in the ways Bodin, Hobbes or Rousseau saw it back in the *Age of Enlightenment.* These times are definitely gone. The world consists today of about *two hundred sovereign nation states,* while at the time it was a handful European hegemonies who were controlling the rest of the world. This gives a totally different picture, and also a different power picture. When powers are differently aligned, sovereignty is relativized, and therefore must be redefined, because sovereignty is power, nothing but power, if one sees that power given by god, by the people or by a parliament doesn't make a difference.

And when we speak about power, we also speak about the power of the individual, which today surely is greater than back in the times of absolutism. In addition, an organization such as the Christian Church that through their power games manipulated and infantilized the masses in the whole of Europe is unthinkable today. Another factor of change is the information flow that today assumed such gigantic proportions that only professional media experts can channel it and provide daily information that is even remotely accurate.

Published by Sirius-C Media Galaxy LLC, 2010

While abuses still occur, and while conflict and wars still are daily reality, the difference is that today every single human on the globe can instantly be informed about them, and can make up their mind about them. This power of information has rarely ever been validated in international textbooks, as international law scholars often are living in ivory towers, which is why their political predictions, if ever they engage in them, are to be taken with a grain of salt. It is different, as a general rule, with *international lawyers* who have seen how law and custom get embroiled in, for example, sovereign immunity litigation, and who know that the often lauded precision of international law is largely a myth. Today, with the rise of the international consumer culture, while there are of course new pitfalls for state power crushing the individual through a blown-up control and supervision machinery, there is potentially and despite all a higher chance for the individual to emerge more powerful than this ever was thinkable in the past. This fact has in my view not yet been validated in international law textbooks, as it's perhaps of a mere psychological nature for the moment, until it will be solidified by paradigm changes and legal reform in the future. In the years to come, the rising political transparence and the fact that power abuses are relatively quickly unveiled and revealed to the public, will gradually disempower the worldwide truthholder conglomerates and emasculate their imperialistic monopolies and favoritism that enriches an oligarchy beyond all measure, while leaving hundreds of millions mentally, materially and spiritually impoverished! On the other hand, new global business opportunities will arise for those who build on freedom and democracy and who listen to the true needs of the masses. While companies that build on privileges or outmoded traditions, a blown-up self-image or that adhere to undemocratic or even tyrannical forms of leadership will be surprised how quickly and effectively the new era will literally wipe them from the surface of international business.

The highest reward will be for those who serve the customer and who build a service-oriented business model that empowers the consumer, that is transparent, that gives options and that is consistent in structure and constant in time.

In this sense, I see consumer culture, with its *network structure* and global scope, as a potentially fertile soil for sovereignty going global in the sense of being transformed into a concept of 'sovereign participation' in a world government that represents the interests of *all humans on the globe*, whatever their cultural, religious, ethnic or social belonging.

I do not dare a prognosis how what Alvin Toffler called *Powershift* will make its way through humanity and how big the damage will be they are going to leave behind in their resistance to the establishment of a new balance, while we all know that the precarious chaotic pseudo-order of the *Second Wave* or antithesis cannot be maintained, or we are all to perish. Toffler sees this transition clearly as a revolutionary and perhaps bloody process, but anyway as a period of intense conflict. In *Powershift (1991)*, Toffler writes:

Alvin Toffler

A revolutionary new system for creating wealth cannot spread without triggering personal, political and international conflict. Change the way wealth is made and

Published by Sirius-C Media Galaxy LLC, 2010

you immediately collide with all the entrenched interests whose power arose from the prior wealth-system.
Bitter conflicts erupt as each side fights for control of
the future.[6]

Those who fought for control of the future made use
of violence, wealth, and knowledge. Today a similar,
though far more accelerated, upheaval has started.
The changes we have recently seen in business, the
economy, politics, and at the global level are only the
first skirmishes of far bigger power struggles to come.
For we stand at the edge of the deepest powershift in
human history.[7]

The Empowered Citizen

The Citizen Redefined

Back in 1998, I was invited to Brunei, the small kingdom in South-East Asia, for a presentation to the Ministry of Interior; they were interested in a leadership training for their civil servants. To be true, I was not little surprised about the forward-thinking attitude of these generally rather conservative Muslim leaders. The seminar, I was told, should take the form of a *train-the-trainers* program, so as to give a totally new shape to their formation of all civil servants in the country. As I had done such a training formerly for the government of Indonesia, they were interested in recruiting me as a trainer. When we first sat at the meeting table, a department head of the Ministry of Interior held a short speech for opening the discussion. After a short polite introduction and welcome, he said this:

– We see that in the past, the civil servant was the murky, obedient and often brutal executive who would carry things through to the end, even if he's wrong, thereby often hurting citizens and making for a bad image of the government. We know that *we do not want* this kind of civil servant for the future! We think that today the citizen is not anymore the vassal of their government, but the *customer* of the government. Accordingly, we need a civil servant who is responsive, alert, civilized, humble, courteous, respectful and smart, and who lets our government appear as positive and caring in the eyes of our people. Can you help us to get there?

Published by Sirius-C Media Galaxy LLC, 2010

I was humbled. Never would I have expected such a progressive position from the government of a country that on the international scene comes over as a political tyranny, with a 98% Muslim population, a powerful and perhaps despotic ruler family, and an administration that is so opaque that most journalists say they ignore the details when they report any news in the country. And I had to acknowledge that our image of foreign states is so often veiled by prejudice and by quick judgments, while a culture, a society, a nation is a very complex thing, actually a living thing, an *organism* – not a machine. It is obvious for any political observer today that nation states that formerly were known only to diplomats and international scholars, today can make big headlines with their extraordinary ideas.

Whatever the image is that the world puts upon them, the reality may be very different. In other words, we are so accustomed to the best ideas emerging from our famous European and American universities that we often overlook to see them appear in a different cultural, social and political setting. This may be humbling us at first sight, but we really have to get used to it because it will be the political reality of tomorrow.

The World Model Revisited

The European model, as we are going to see in this monograph, has only a limited validity. It has the validity of a 'primal scene', so to speak, for a world government of the future, the validity of a model that was for the time being a good and necessary solution. But fact is that Europe, at that time, was seen as 'the world', because of their Colonial powers; this was also a fact of international law. But international law has changed since then, and the world today is not anymore represented by Europe and European 'world politics'. Today world politics is global politics, and while the power and economic structures of course are still dictated by a few superpowers, this picture is currently changing.

It was quite visible during the economic crisis in 2008/2009 that nations that still some decades ago were treated as 'poor developing countries' had almost no negative effects in that crisis that ravaged European and American banks, businesses and private consumers.

In India, there was only a slight turndown, and Cambodia, the country where I live and work since more than six years and where I am writing this book, had as good as no contrary effects. One of the reasons for this astonishing situation is that Cambodia does do not yet have a stock market; another reason is that Cambodia is not indebted; the country has received huge amounts of money for restructuring their economy after the Khmer Rouge disaster, but that money was given unconditionally, not in the form of loans.

While this information never appeared anywhere in the headlines, it is significant to see that the reverse effects of large global crises may hit those most who have accumulated a lot of bad karma in the past, because of their oppressive and colonialist politics, and we are going to see small countries emerging more and more who will come up with new and original solutions and will reap great benefits when they

Published by Sirius-C Media Galaxy LLC, 2010

can manage their resources and give real service to their citizens, and other nations's citizens they want to attract for bestowing upon them those services. For example, Cambodia has become a fine banking economy, with modern banks set in place, with a strong Central Bank that is modeled after the German central bank, that tightly supervises and controls all Cambodian banks, so that a maximum amount of safety is guaranteed for foreign investments and deposits.

Economolitics

This being said, the restriction of national sovereignty as a project that may take *several more decades* for being accomplished, cannot be seen in a vacuum; it has to be seen as embedded in those structural changes that transform national economies to be more and more entangled with each other, more and more networked, more and more electronic and fluid, more and more volatile, ad hoc, 'mobile' and more and more transparent and 'unpolitical'. It is an old fact that a free economy fosters communication and intercourse between peoples of different cultures, and thereby turns against religious and political fundamentalism. This fact is notorious for example in how Venice was ruled by the Doges, how rich they became, how independent from the Vatican, and how much this has benefited Venice, and Venetian lifestyle and culture. It was, compared to the Church-ruled other regions in Italy, a free lifestyle, with refined pleasures and arts being on top of the agenda. This can actually be seen as an early form of a *secular government* as it later became the model for the modern state, such as France, during the Renaissance, which is perhaps the prototype model.

Growing Child Power

Legal efforts to reform the *laws of consent* have been considered in all major industrial nations even though not much change has been implemented yet. You may ask what laws of consent have to do with world economy, international law and world peace? Well, quite a lot. The child is considered as a major business participant since about the second half of the 17th century. Children were needed in the *Industrial Revolution* as certain tasks, such as for example weaving fine textures, could only be executed, at that time, with using the small hands of a child. Children, from that time, were cruelly exploited, so rampantly actually that it triggered a dramatic change in the child-rearing paradigm. After some years of this abject economic and also sexual child abuse going in the land in the major European capitals, a resistance movement was making itself felt, first through pointed conferences, and later through national and international cooperation, and a paradigm was formed that was later called 'child protection' and that was at first inspired for protecting children from child labor and from sexual exploitation.

This form of protection took quite a long time to become effective because of the poverty of the masses and the financial power of the industrial power holders, but by and by the conditions of the child worker improved, until eventually child labor was declared illegal in all Western industrial

Published by Sirius-C Media Galaxy LLC, 2010

nations. From about the 19th century to today, the power of the child as a consumer has risen, in that the industry targets children as their main adressees for publicity; however, at the same time the *power of the child as a full human* has drastically declined because the child is not so far being granted free choice relations, with the result that they see their intimacy and erotic experiences curtailed down for complying with the needs of the industry to become *prime consumers.*

This is about where we are at this moment. But I predict a further change, adaptation or expansion of the global consumer paradigm in that the child, given their privileged position in the economy, will be granted *more power* in the future, and that means also, the power to have free choice relations, and to have a complete sexual life.

I admit that the resistance is strong to that idea, not because of any so-called *morality concept*, which at present really is a fiction, but because of the necessity for the present consumer paradigm to change in order to match up with the growing power needs of children and adolescents. The resistance to considering the child a full human is not a morality demand. Genuine morality, which is founded upon respect of the difference of another fosters paradigms that are socially and sexually permissive. In native cultures around the world, it can be seen that genuine morality and spirituality does foster the emotional and sexual freedom of children, and their early autonomy and self-reliance. It can be seen in these native cultures that parent-child emotional entanglement as we experience it as the rule in our modern consumer economies is actually a perversion from the natural continuum.

Children today, in our modern economies, have the right and the power to have their laptops and ipods and they can browse more or less freely the Internet and can get their own information, instead of being restricted to the official media in form of national televisions, as this was still the case when I myself was a young boy.

This alone gives them a tremendous power boost, while this power boost is hardly matched by the current educational paradigm that is still stuck in the past, with its insistence upon discipline, obedience and social compliance. But most youngsters today go their own ways, and they develop their own creativity. This is an obvious fact of life today anywhere on the Internet.

I am now in my fifties and get comments to my Youtube channel from little boys or girls aged ten to fifteen, on a regular basis, be it they are child prodigies, and are interested in my coaching services for pianists, or because they have their own unique political and social opinions and wish to voice them. In general, my Youtube statistics showed me that my main audience is just 13 to 18, with only a few older people for some of my videos. This fact honestly surprised me to a point it got me to deeply reflect on today's consumer economy and who actually drives it. I came to believe that children and adolescents in a way drive our economy and that is why, logically so, they are going to be empowered in the near and far future, and that the 'child protection' laws are going to be changed to their favor − and not, as many believe, for doing a favor to pedophiles, for we encounter here clearly two different policy agendas. I believe that the *pedophile agenda*

Published by Sirius-C Media Galaxy LLC, 2010

is a *fake agenda* as there is only *one* agenda that drives us forward as a society today, it's the child's agenda, not the child-lover's agenda. It's the agenda of mother nature, that requires respecting the female and the child as part of the *female creator energy*, not the male dominator energy that was the reigning paradigm during the hubristic madness of patriarchy.

A Changing Social Framework

The discussion is ongoing. I am convinced that the future will bring real changes here because the present new generations need to grow up for implementing them. There will be more rights for elders, too, and a *more acute awareness* of the precious wisdom of elders through their communication and togetherness with children, as this was realized by Françoise Dolto in the 1980s in Paris, France.[8]

The young modern citizen simply feels more empowered to boycott social collaboration each and every time personal freedom is curtailed down by laws and regulations. This new citizen will more easily become a social reformer who doesn't shy away from contacting their president or senators for making social policy suggestions.

This also means that many of the existing forms of social police and denunciation that are undermining personal freedom and trust between people will be abandoned for allowing humanity to develop into a more trustful state of togetherness. It will be seen that peace can only be based upon *freedom, trust and abundant soul power of the individual,* and not upon ruthless competition, endless social and economical hierarchies, oligarchy, tyranny and persecution. In fact, our mass media do all to prevent world citizens to gain this awareness as our present economies, and their marketing philosophies, are built upon the idea of the 'national state'.

However, this monolithic structure is currently eroding more and more with the economic reality of a 'networked' world economy, where national segments are more and more intertwined with each other, and where the general entanglement becomes one of global dimensions. It is obvious that the more our national economies are entangled with each other, the lesser are chances that because of national sovereignty conflicts, huge wars will be engaged, simply because the 'winners' and 'losers' can hardly be anticipated, and the danger of 'being hurt' when 'hurting others' becomes a real global concern. It's as if we were all living together today in a huge elevator, and when we begin to shoot around, the danger is not just that we kill each other, but that the whole elevator will crash down.

The Rights of Ethnic, Social and Sexual Minorities

When the transition from authority-based economies to *functional network economies* will be the order of the day, the concept of 'minority' will assume a quite different meaning as it had in the past. It is no wonder that in a social system that sanctifies the power of the majority, the *in-group*, as the Bible reports it, there is huge individual and collective aggression toward the *out-group*. This will be very different in

Published by Sirius-C Media Galaxy LLC, 2010

the economies that are ahead of us and that are going to implement the leading economic paradigm of the future. In these economies, the division between *in* and *out* is no more valid as a *survival paradigm*, that it was indeed in ancient times, for the simple reason that today the survival paradigm of the future is the integrative solution that *embraces the difference* of the other, in that it embraces the whole of the market place.

When the market place is *global*, this means that there is no other solution than a *global humanity* on both the economical and the political levels. This new integrative and holistic paradigm, that of course got its major incentive from our integrative and holistic science, will automatically integrate cultural and ethnic dividers, and it will 'rationalize' all religious diversion to come to see the unity in diversity, and the diversity in unity.

This, then, will be the start of a global culture that is able to embrace and develop the idea of a *world government* as the ultimate solution for bringing us world peace.

An Uncanny International Organization

I am going to have a look at an *uncanny international organization* that was so far not being considered as such, yet which has the potential to help bringing about a democratic world government in the future. I am talking about the World Wide Web, the information highway, the Internet.

It seems to me that human intelligence which created the Internet is fundamentally different from all what we had before in human history. The interesting fact about it is that not one man or woman has created it, but many, often simultaneously cooperating from different points of the globe. The Web was thus perhaps the first really effective global institution we have created. And that is why, among other reasons that I believe the Internet will grow beyond an information highway to become a *political highway* as well. When we compare the Internet with another global institution, the United Nations, there are at least two striking differences.

The United Nations was a creation of states, at a government level, and not something growing from the base layer of societies. The privileges or advantages that the UN provides were primarily intended for the *principi*, the former kings or rulers, and later for the nation states. Let us not forget the fact that for the protection of the individual, international law still provides only a minimum standard. Human rights and the rights of minority populations are protected *only within the range of special pacts or agreements,* such as the international conventions against torture, yet the nation states are free to join these international agreements or not.

The second, perhaps more important point of difference is that the United Nations, after their creation, have pretty much split into regional power groups. It's not a coincidence that the European Community was another branch of the same tree, coming out of vision that people like Woodrow Wilson and, as we shall see further down, even philosophers like Rousseau and Kant had about the future of a united world. At the same time, *European Integration* was pouring wine into the water of the original idea of a *Community of Nations* that is truly global.

Published by Sirius-C Media Galaxy LLC, 2010

That is why I believe the Internet is an *extraordinary creation,* for it has a far-reaching political potential. It is as if it had been created by an unconscious will, something like a *cosmic intention* that is beyond a merely human perspective.

When you observe the development of the Web and the fact that really Mr. Everyone and Ms. Shareware drive it forward to set new cultural and commercial standards, you can but be amazed about the power of the individual.

This may sound provocative. Yet we touch here a mystery that goes beyond all what we have observed hitherto on the globe, something that is like a new gospel, a new power, and a new global village for all.

So, to put it clearly, the Internet is the first international organization that really works in the sense of *res publica,* as the old Romans called political matters. And in that sense, as a forum for the public cause, the Internet really is *functional.*

Minorities, for example, be they racial, political or sexual, are effectively propagated through the Web. The police laws of most countries can prohibit minorities from gathering as long as the gatherings take place within local boundaries. But the police cannot legally control them when these gatherings are held online.

Since Web meetings are virtual, they do not fall within those laws. As a result it can be said that the Web created more democracy and freedom of speech.

However, this freedom also means that we have to use it responsibly. If we allow people to abuse of it, we jeopardize our newly gained privilege. International fundamentalism, secret services, right-wing movements, misguided groupings and a large mass of frustrated and negative individuals only wait for the chance to exert a tight control over the Web so as to install new and hitherto unknown forms of totalitarian government and rulership. The only effective way to prevent this from happening is that we exert responsible self-control in all forms of online publishing and virtual communication. This implies that we have to become conscious of the value that is linked to freedom and to simple and unprejudiced human communication.

Instead, people seem to ask for more regulation and strict guidelines for conduct on the virtual space. This is however within the old paradigm. It means to restrict freedom once again because a certain amount of frivolous people are unable to use it responsibly. If we want to avoid this result, we have only one choice, either to provide organizations with set regulations inviting people to become members for set purposes and to limit communication to set purposes and for set interests or topics, or to change the paradigm. What is presently taking place on the Web is the first alternative. It means basically to create cages for people who have not learned to conduct themselves properly outside of those cages, and in full freedom. Human history was an up and down of times of more and less freedom. But at all times certain people have searched for cages because they were afraid of freedom or abused of it to the detriment of all.

However, it's not that difficult to live in wild life. While nature basically regulates itself automatically, by a process called *self-regulation*. I believe self-regulation, which has been found by systems research to be one of the most basic and

Published by Sirius-C Media Galaxy LLC, 2010

most functional ingredients of living systems, will become a social and even a political value.

Now, let's shift our perspective from the economical to the political and have a closer look at that daring idea of the Web becoming, perhaps not too far in the future, a real *international organization and political forum* of all peoples in the world. We know from the development of the European Union (EU) that the political union is very difficult to realize, and in fact the EU is far from being a political union with all what this would involve for its member states. The reason is probably that so much trustbuilding is required for a large number of people agreeing on implementing new systems of government or conceding national powers to a supranational organism.

The United Nations is a striking example for how *not to do it correctly.* They were from the beginning set to implement a political unification with, in the future, ideally, a world government. However, the anxieties were and are so high that the courageous goals were pursued less than half-heartedly. The end result was that bad compromises were made, compromises that really were compromising the whole idea and led to an absurd reality which counts as its major fact the largest bureaucracy in the world, engendering an irresponsible waste of resources.

But let me ask, where is the Web heading? You may object that it is too far-fetched to admit that the Web could eventually bring about what both the European Union and the United Nations did not achieve: a world community, a union of nations, of peoples. How can?

If we take a closer look at this seemingly Utopian idea, we see that there is a fundamental difference between the European Union and the United Nations, on one hand, and the Web, on the other, in their respective ways to realize this global union of peoples. The difference is the fact that the Web begins at the basis whereas all other present international organizations began at the top. What do I mean?

On the Web, masses of people from different cultures get into communicating with each other, first for research or academic purposes, then for business, the exchange of goods and services, and eventually for simply getting to know each other, looking at one another's home pages, learning from each other, communicating basic needs, feelings and opinions. The trend is that the Web becomes every day more a meeting place for a *large variety of people* communicating for a *large variety of purposes*. While in the beginning the user had to write out every single command, with the graphic interface of the World Wide Web things became really simple and intuitive. In the meantime, also nonliterate people are able to write: they'll just talk and the computer will write for them.

I already pointed out that existing international organizations, despite the fact that they were instituted to unify peoples, have begun their work with the top classes of society, the rulers, kings and later the sovereign states, and not really six billion individuals. If we build a house from the roof, forgetting about its foundation, its basis, the house will crash before it is ready. This is the true reason why neither the European Union nor the United Nations accomplish in reality what they have been created for: it's simply because they

Published by Sirius-C Media Galaxy LLC, 2010

were established as *roof structures with a pitiful lack of foundation*. They came about through governmental collaboration and agreements, and not as a result of the will and the work of the peoples who have set these governments in place. They have not grown from the base layer of society, but from its top range.

That is why I am convinced that the Web will be the foundation for the *true union of peoples* in not too distant a future. The Web grew without any governmental control, although it was, paradoxically, created for governmental purposes. Yet from the moment it was given to the public by the military agencies that had created it, it was a free landscape for new discoveries. And it quickly grew beyond national borders and cultures.

My idea may seem uncanny. Consider that also on the national level, stability was reached only from the moment that the peoples themselves chose their governments. This is not so much a function of the constitutional system which can be monarchical or republican. As long as a king or ruler is firmly based upon the trust of his people, his government will bring about effective solutions and bear fruits. Some of the old Chinese kings who based their rulership upon the true interest of their people and universal laws have given abundant evidence to this historical and political fact. On the other hand, the best republican government that is corrupt and has lost the trust of a majority of citizens will disappear sooner or later and leave a vacuum of frustration and a bad taste in the mouth of the populace.

What only counts is that the system is truly democratic, which means not just democratic on paper. On both the national and the international level, democracy brings about stability. Governments who do not enjoy the backup of their peoples reign in *instable conditions* and can be thrown over by social unrest and upheaval.

Present international organizations are for the great majority established 'from above', without democratic elections from the side of the peoples, in a process that is not transparent to the citizen. This is one of the reasons why the 'man in the street', be it in the West or the East, when asked about the United Nations or similar organizations, either admits ignorance and gives a negative or indifferent judgment. This is simply so, and understandable because they have not been directly involved in the creation of the organization or the election of its staff. How can these organizations then seriously attempt to build a future world government?

They would reign over people who do not even know them. Therefore, if these organizations, as it seems now, are unable to allow reforms, they will disappear.

This is in part also valid for the European Union. That is why a few years ago the *European Parliament* was fundamentally reformed and direct elections for the European parliamentarians have been institutionalized. In the public opinion all over Europe this step was considered as a progress of the unification progress, although skepticism prevailed as to how the European Union will practically carry out the will of the peoples at its basis, and not only the will of their governments or top-class industrials.

Published by Sirius-C Media Galaxy LLC, 2010

The Web has grown from the root up, and not from the branches down, as all present political international organizations did. Therefore, the chance that my prediction will come true is, I think, higher than the chance that it will not.

For it is much easier and much more effective to learn a healthy body perform more functions than to teach a sick and dysfunctional body to perform even very few basic functions. And the present international organizations are not only sick and dysfunctional, they waste human and financial resources to an extent that their maintenance equals ruin for all those who, willingly or unwillingly, have to finance them. And that is all of us.

CHAPTER TWO

The *United States of Europe*, Utopia or Future Reality?

Introduction

In this first chapter we are going to see that the idea of world government, of a unification of peoples, and for the purpose of bringing peace is not new. It was contained in the so-called *peace plans* drafted by European philosophers back in the 18th century; since then, the unification idea has fueled a constant progress toward peace and peaceful cooperation among European countries.

For all those who are still critical about Europe, the fact should be considered that since 1945, there was no more war between the nations that are members of the *European Union (EU)* and the treaties that preceded the union, the *ECSC (1951)* and the *EEC (1957)*.

While the European integrative process was surely not smooth, and while there is still much to criticize, the unification of Europe was successful by and large, and it has given peace to peoples who formerly were constantly battling with each other.

We are going to see in this chapter that the major problem in world politics is not the racial, ethnic or cultural difference of peoples, but the institution of *national sovereignty*, as a power structure that is very much prone to being abused.

Interestingly enough, this was seen by those European philosophers, Kant, Rousseau, and others already after about *the first two hundred years* of national sovereignty having become a doctrine in international law. It was from about the 16th century, with the decline of the Church's power during the

Renaissance, and with the need to form strong secular governments that the doctrine was gradually set in place, in the main European nations, Germany, France and Italy. Generally, the publication of Machiavelli's political novel *The Prince (1513)*, is seen by international law scholars as a mark stone for the establishment of the *doctrine of national sovereignty* in international law and practice.

Until the 18th century, it had become obvious to political observers and realistic philosophers that the doctrine of national sovereignty, and the mere fact that those modern governments were secular for the most part, did not bring the desired benefits. One of the initial ideas behind the establishment of strong secular governments was to avoid religious wars that had devastated Europe during the Middle-Ages, and under the politically flawed regime of the Church. The idea was indeed that national sovereignty would bring more peace, by avoiding religious conflicts, wars and civil wars.

But it was unfortunately a shortsighted view for each of those strong secular regimes, then, wanted to gain the overhand in Europe, with the result that warfare continued, and became even more devastating than ever before in Europe. And we all know that it continued all through the centuries until 1945!

Thus, we can say Europe is an interesting forum for testing ideas, and we can conclude, contrary to the many black seers today, that the idea of unification was bringing peace to Europe without destroying national identities, cultures, languages and customs.

Published by Sirius-C Media Galaxy LLC, 2010

In fact, this is the main argument among today's youth against the idea of world government; they fear that a unification of the globe would lead to an Orwellian global system that would suppress personal freedom and lead to a kind of global Nazi empire. The voices are strong, and one has to browse only Google, Youtube and other popular forums to see what young people today think of the idea.

It seems to me that *conspiracy theory* has become so popular that at the end of the day, it's difficult to make out what is reality and what is conspiracy. In fact, these masses of people have rarely looked over the fence of their own cultural, political and social conditioning, and they have rarely investigated the details of human political history. If they had, they would see that war, while it's triggered by political and economic greed, is regularly sold to the masses with psychological arguments that stress the *difference* of the other nation, and that paint that other reality in blacker notes than that one is familiar with.

This was very well visible in the history of World War II, where about every nation involved in the war game indulged in *demonizing the other nations,* those on 'the other side', while painting rosy images for those nations one was allied with.

The masses rarely know what the real motivations are for triggering wars, and who actually gains all that money with war; what they get to see and to hear is the psychological rhetoric that targets at demonizing those one wishes to attack and subdue. This argument is valid both for what at that time was called by Hitler 'the outer enemy' and 'the inner enemy'.

The rhetoric of the Nazis was namely to demonize the Jews as the main 'inner enemies', which is the strategy that eventually resulted in the Holocaust. Thus, it has to be seen that the main danger in all of this is that people do not really know who are those beyond the fence, what kind of people they are, what they think and do, what they believe to be true, and so forth. They imagine them to be 'very different', just because of their lacking knowledge about them, and that is why they can easily be brought to believe that those others are 'evil' or 'more evil' than oneself. It is no wonder then that people who enjoyed higher education, and who have traveled much, who speak different languages, are seldom manipulated into becoming haters and persecutors, or war mangers. It is always those who know little, who have seen and heard little, and who ignore the main truths about the commonality of all human beings, as a matter of cosmic resonance, as a matter of the basic harmony within all of creation. The war mangers exploit that lack of knowledge of the masses, to get them where the political and economic leaders want to get them, and this manipulatory process is much more difficult to stage *once peoples are unified in one land* without national borders, without passport controls, and without national newspapers that use to emphasize the 'goodness' of one's nation and their people, and the 'strangeness' of the other nations and their people.

The argument that 'national identities' have to be preserved is a fallacy. It is exactly that hypothetical and illusory fiction of national identity that leads to all those wars. There is no such identity, and if there is, *it has been put up as a matter of*

Published by Sirius-C Media Galaxy LLC, 2010

constant ruthless propaganda, for the very purpose of leading the people to the next war. People have customs, they have personal, ethnic, religious and regional identities, they may have clan identities as well, as one can see in Italy or Corsica, they certainly have cultural identities, but not by nature a national identity. Hence, the harmful element is the national identity because it is the psychological mirror of national sovereignty.

When national sovereignty is voluntarily restricted by the nation states member of a world government, national identities will be gone if not from one day to the other, but within a few months or years, they will be dissolved, while the other identities will be kept in place.

It may be useful during the first years of such a government to actively emphasize the cultural identities of the peoples, in the sense a Hopi native recently communicated it to me. He said that the Hopi idea of peaceful togetherness was indeed one where there is 'diversity within unity', and that their leaders, when they emphasize peace and unity, always also emphasize the cultural diversity of the different tribes.

The Early Plans for 'Eternal Peace'

It has been observed since the beginning of the Iraq invasion that the political weight of the European Union (EU) and the process of *European Integration* were never before of greater and more global importance than at that moment in human political history.

In fact, had the union reached not only a certain amount of economic integration but also *political integration* with a central European government and an established foreign politics, the outcome of USA's offensive war declaration against Iraq might have been different.[9]

As the leading socioeconomic and political powers in present-day Europe, led by France and Germany, were and are against a unilateral world-policing superpower USA that forces each and every opponent or pseudo-opponent to knee-jerking 'world democracy', a third political power block next to America and Asia, however it may be called, represents a potentially paradigm-shifting lever for bringing about a large-scale landslide on the political and strategic world map.

It is a well-known fact that France under a courageous and self-assured President Jacques Chirac played a particularly preponderant role in contradicting George W. Bush's foreign policy concept for the Middle East, unveiling it as a badly masked invasion strategy with a neocolonial base intention. It makes a fundamental difference when on the international scene not a single nation state dares to oppose the United States' hegemonic world power, but a whole political,

Published by Sirius-C Media Galaxy LLC, 2010

economic and military block of two dozens of nation states. This block that a politically unified Europe could represent in the future, is of amazingly similar dimensions as the United States, both in terms of size and economic prowess. And the people who drafted these peace projects were no lesser than the greatest philosophers of Europe, or perhaps of humanity, and they certainly are considered as highly integer by United States citizens as well.

In this sub-chapter, I shall have a look at what historically were the common roots of both the process of *supranational* and of *international* integration. Many today seem to have forgotten that the original impetus for founding a united Europe was first of all to establish an international political system suited for purporting peace, stability and growth for *all nation states,* regardless of their military might and their economic and political power.

The early peace projects were unanimously targeting at bringing about a new era of peace, nothing less and nothing of lesser value for all of us, that is, for the world community, not just for Europe. It is important to note this as the starting point, because it shows the human, and truly international intention of the early fathers of the world peace idea.

I will first present the peace projects drafted by Abbé de Saint-Pierre, Jean-Jacques Rousseau, Immanuel Kant, Saint-Simon and Coudenhove-Kalergi that were intended at bringing about a European confederation – of whatever structure and political form – with the single most important focus to facilitate the peace process between nation states that historically have always fought against each other.

That is why these plans or projects for a *European Constitution* are simply called 'peace plans' in the international law literature. And when we consider the quite notorious international debate on the occasion of the invasion of the United States in Iraq, we cannot close our eyes in front of the political reality that a historical chance for establishing a peaceful world community has been missed at the onset of the 21st century. It was hopefully not missed forever.

Published by Sirius-C Media Galaxy LLC, 2010

Abbé de Saint-Pierre

The peace plan of the French Abbé de Saint-Pierre, pre-sented in his *Mémoire pour Rendre la Paix Perpétuelle en Europe (1713)*, literally translated as *Memo for Establishing Eternal Peace in Europe*, foresaw a 'Confederation of all European Sovereigns'. The unified Europe was projected to be directed by a federal government.[10] This plan stipulated in its five main articles that –

▸ Representatives of the contracting member states are going to be members of a permanent congress;

▸ The number of the voting sovereigns and those that are invited to join the convention is to be established;

▸ Each member state is to receive a guarantee safeguarding his territorial property; by the same token, the sovereign, his family and his premises are to be protected both against foreign invaders and rebellion from the side of his own vassals;

▸ The congress is functioning as the highest judge regarding the rights of the member states;

▸ The community is to be enabled to proceed with armed forces against each and every member state that breaks the convention, as well as against public enemies.[11]

This early plan already contained the idea of creating a *supranational authority* to be assigned precisely outlined powers and competences, while it must be conceded that these competences were in last resort depending on the goodwill of the sovereigns member of the convention. Obviously, the guarantee of each sovereign's personal and territorial power seemed to have been the main focus of the draft convention. Interestingly, we know through historical research that this point (point three of the draft convention) was added later to the draft by Abbé de Saint-Pierre, namely in the hope of giving a stimulus to sovereigns to join the convention.

Published by Sirius-C Media Galaxy LLC, 2010

Jean-Jacques Rousseau

The project of a European government was a preoccupation of no lesser a mind than Jean-Jacques Rousseau. He discussed the plan of Abbé de Saint-Pierre in his draft convention entitled *Extrait du Projet de Paix Perpétuelle de Monsieur l'Abbé de Saint-Pierre (1761).*[12] Starting from a rather pessimistic outlook on the will of European sovereigns to ratify such a wide-ranging supranational agreement, thereby renouncing up some of their sovereignty, he wrote in 1758 in the *Fragment sur le Projet de Paix Perpétuelle:*

Jean-Jacques Rousseau

One must be as simple-minded as Abbé de Saint-Pierre for proposing the slightest innovation in whatever government in the world ...[13]

Rousseau argued that common sense or 'reason' was not enough to ban future wars[14] and instead required a clear and unequivocal subordination of the partner states under the newly created supranational federal government in exactly the same way as individuals are subordinated to their home country's government.[15] And that Rousseau's ideas were not bleak and blank propositions, but had realistic impact is to be seen in the precise wording of the conditions that Rousseau puts on paper:

> ▸ A federal government with singular and precise competencies;

> ▸ A federal legislation that is directly binding;

> ▸ A federal executive power with coercive competence over member states;

> ▸ A cohesion of the confederation so high that in the long run federal interests are going to prevail over national interests.[16]

Rousseau summarizes the advantages of the project in eight points, among which the points five till eight merit particular attention:

> ▸ freedom of trade as well as safety in the trade between member states;

> ▸ reduction of the defense budget and economic gain in times of peace;

> ▸ advancement of agriculture and prosperity for the member states' rulers.[17]

Rousseau proved to be particularly lucid with regard to the details of Abbé de Saint-Pierre's peace convention, but argued that 'the thousand little difficulties will eventually all be levied when an enterprise of this grandeur is going to be put in practice.'[18]

He also recognized a crucial point that today we learn thoroughly in our practice of drafting supranational agreements, namely that it is, if ever, not a coercive force, but the nation states themselves that restrain their sovereignty to convey that supranational or international organism a sovereignty of its own. Rousseau was realistic enough to consider that modern nation states, despite the obvious advantages of supranational agreements, are very reluctant in practice to make concessions with regard to their sovereignty and the privileges it confers.

In his posthumous published writing *Jugement sur le Projet de Paix Perpétuelle (1782)*, Rousseau reflects about the possible interests that nation states might bring in play. And he distinguished between a real and an apparent interest *(intérêt réel et intérêt apparent)* in those states' political action.

Rousseau saw the 'real interest' realized when a peace convention was eventually ratified; the 'apparent interest' was the secret wish of every single sovereign involved in the negotiations to gain privileges and advantages that the others are deprived of. The reason for this ambiguity was, according to Rousseau, the feudal system which made him conclude that a supranational federal government was, if ever, to be brought about through a *revolution*.[19]

This means that, ultimately, Rousseau doubted that the nation states would deliberately, and voluntarily, renounce a large part of their sovereignty for the creation of a world government; he rather speculated that the latter would, if ever, be brought about through chaos, upheaval, and violent transformation of the political status quo.

Immanuel Kant

The German philosopher Immanuel Kant published his peace project *Zum Ewigen Frieden* in 1795, during the last days of the French Revolution.[20] This is a suspicious coincidence when you remember what Jean-Jacques Rousseau had predicted as a condition for world peace. The first two articles of this draft read:

▸ The constitution in all member states shall be republican.[21]

▸ International law is to be based upon a confederation of free states.[22]

It is interesting to read about a European confederation for the first time not in 1951, but in 1795 and thus one hundred fifty years before the first step of *European Integration* that still today, at the time I write this, in 2010, is not entirely realized, as we have *not yet reached political unification.*

We should have a closer look at these two main articles of Kant's convention. What is highly interesting, even from today's perspective, is the fact that Kant recognized what might be called the *internal setup of the member states* (Article 1) to be equally important as their togetherness on the international stage (Article 2). The internal setup, the 'constitutional software' as it were of a nation state is what Kant considered to be the hanger of the whole convention.

We have had enough experience to know today that indeed without a democratic base setup within each member

Published by Sirius-C Media Galaxy LLC, 2010

state, their peaceful togetherness is highly unlikely. We have good historical examples for the lucidity of this view when we look at Europe, on one hand, and the United States, on the other. The United States realized the *Republican Constitution* within the first state member of the new confederation, after the break with England. This first state of the confederation, nomen est omen, was *New England.*

The creation of the United States of America, with all the prosperity and power this creation was going to bring to its citizens and the world, was possible because all member states were modeled after the prototype of New England, and thus got *state constitutions* with clearly defined civil rights and constitutional guarantees for the citizen.

What happened in Europe? War.

Kant and Rousseau were right in that the feudal system was incompatible with the European unification process; what happened was that the social injustice inherent in feudalism rendered every attempt for peace an illusion for a long time to come.

When we see what cruel and destructive wars were to occur after Kant's and Rousseau's death in Europe until 1945, we get an idea of how painful, slow, incremental and important the unification process was for Europe, until today.

Behold, Kant and Rousseau did not have utopian ideas! Ideas are seeds that fall on soil that is either fertile or not. And often in history ideas fall in soil that is not fertile at the time the ideas come up. As with time and effort, the field was again and again plowed, the soil became more and more fertile, until one day the seed was able to grow. It's like that with all ideas, so why should it have been different with the great idea of a unified Europe?

Today, matters look not bad after all. We have achieved to bring about a *European Union (EU)* with more than forty members and considerable economic power. This union was peaceful since 1945 and thus, what was a rare exception in pre-20th century Europe, there were no more internal wars since sixty-five years. Furthermore, efforts are presently made to draft a directly binding *European Constitution*, which admittedly failed in the first run but that will eventually succeed with the growing insight in the enormous responsibility that we all bear for bringing about this important step toward peace in European history, and by extension and analogy, in world history.

To summarize, when we compare Kant's project with the draft conventions of Abbé de Saint-Pierre and Rousseau, we can say that the French and Swiss philosophers had a keener and more realistic outlook on the future of Europe, and that their proposals were also of higher practical value, more detailed and more down-to-earth than the somewhat idealistic and high-strung plan Immanuel Kant.

Published by Sirius-C Media Galaxy LLC, 2010

Saint-Simon

Contrary to the previously discussed projects that intended to bring about a unified and pacified Europe through a union of their sovereigns, and thus by forming something like a *supranational government*, the proposal submitted by Saint-Simon was targeting much more at a unification of the *peoples* that were going to form the basis for that European Union. In fact, we can make out two possible ways to bring about a European confederation:

▸ Unification from above, through imposing a supranational government;

▸ Unification from below, through a peaceful democratic union of the peoples.

The plan of Saint-Simon, published in 1814, was to create Europe *from the bottom up*, not from the top down.[23]

The title of the draft suggests a unification and confederation of the *peoples* that form the European soil; the solution was a political union that started at the very root level of society. Such a constitution 'from below', the plan projected, was to start the unification process by creating a European parliament *(parlement européen)*.[24] The idea was that as a matter of analogy, a union of peoples was to be created in much the same way as the union of *one people*. When one nation needed a national parliament with representatives for all its citizens, a unified body of peoples needed a supranational parliament with representatives of all the peoples of the union that was forming the legislative body for the confederation. This requirement that today is fully realized, was indeed inspired by a keen sense of political realities. Saint-Simon concluded that without such a parliament, all, in the future of Europe, was again but a result of the power play of the European rulers.[25]

The plan also contained one of the base principles of an *integrational model,* which is the creation of independent European institutions with precisely described competences.

Saint-Simon, just like Rousseau and Kant, started from the premise that as a first step a republican regime was to be founded in each of the future member states of the confederation. The formulation of this goal in the plan can be taken as the classical functional description of a parliament:

Count Saint-Simon

> There must be a coactive force that unifies the singular intentions, orchestrates the movements, transforms interests as propitious for the common good and solidifies commitments.[26]

Saint-Simon's idea that a European confederation could be created only from the moment that a republican regime was established in each member state is interesting because it predicted the future in some way. We have seen the problem broadly discussed with regard to Turkey's anticipated membership of the European Union. While Turkey has a republican constitution, the human rights abuses that Turkey is internationally blamed for might be an obstacle on both a political and integrational level. The public discussion has made it clear that no member state of the EU is willing to tolerate

Published by Sirius-C Media Galaxy LLC, 2010

a state-member that openly or in hidden ways sabotages civil rights or fosters totalitarian ways of government.

The difference to the setup of the United Nations is striking here as under the United Nations Charter, the form and nature of the internal government of each member state would belong to the 'internal affairs of that state' and thus not justify any action from the part of the other members states, Art. 2 (4) United Nations Charter. This is a good example to show how different the United Nations are from the European Union in that European Integration was from the start understood as a process that requires *a much higher level of coherence and homogeneity* from its member states than, for example, the United Nations.

Another point of interest in discussing Saint-Simon's plan is the biting criticism of the peace project by Abbé de Saint-Pierre. Joining Rousseau in the reproach that the priest's proposal was to rigidify and perpetuate the feudal system, there are four points that Saint-Simon derives from the Church's organization:

▸ A unified conception of *national and supranational* governmental structures and competences;

▸ A total independence of the supranational government from the national governments;

▸ Motivation of the supranational government should be rooted exclusively in common interests, and not in partial interests of certain member states;

▸ Public opinion within the community as the only guide post for the action of supranational government and parliament representatives.[27]

These maxims are of an astounding lucidity and have not lost a bit of their originality to this very day. In fact they are fully valid and applicable still in our present societies, and we can observe that they are often not respected in the daily running of the European Union.

Only in one point Saint-Simon's view was a bit too limitative. He saw the function of the European Parliament exclusively in resolving conflicts between member states, overlooking that the main function of a parliament is its legislative power, and that conflict resolution traditionally is better placed in the hands of diplomacy and direct personal contacts between head of states. But apart from this single limitation, Saint-Simon's plan is of high value and has certainly given flesh to the present integration model.

In addition, and contrary to Abbé de Saint-Pierre, Rousseau and Kant, Saint-Simon saw the functional and dynamic character of European Integration, its constancy and incremental character characterized by moving from one stage of integration to the next.

He saw the beginning of the confederation in a union of the British and French parliaments to *one common parliament,* in which at a later stage the German parliament should join.

This was historically the first time that the idea of a *gradual process* of European integration was invented and elaborated, and we can clearly see today that this idea was the one that was going to be realized in Europe from 1951 until to-

Published by Sirius-C Media Galaxy LLC, 2010

day, and not Rousseau's extravagant idea of bringing about peace and stability through a bloody revolution.

The aftermath of the French Revolution, as we all know, has shown that in fact the feudal structures were only labeled differently but that in substance nothing changed – only that many people lost their lives for an idiotic political reform that decapitated undesired heads only to put even more undesired heads in their place. But the French revolution and also the German revolution of 1848 taught European self-thinkers and honest politicians that a unification of Europe was not going to be brought about through revolutions, bloody or unbloody, but through gradual change, flexible renewal, constant good-will and a step-by-step process of social, economic and political *integration*.

Today, every single head of state in Europe is convinced of this reality, and this insight makes the strength of Europe, and to a much lesser extent our economic or future political power. We have grown from our sandbox games into more mature relationships, and such a process can only create results through deep reflection and a strong effort to putting the past behind, not through quick-tempered decisions and emotional turmoil.

And this poised condition and self-assured outlook into the future is mirrored in the Charter of the EEC, Art. 237, 1 where we read that *'every European state can apply for membership in the community'*.

Coudenhove-Kalergi

After the catastrophe of World War I, and in a situation where a keen sense of realities replaced 19th century idealism a new voice was to be heard that was fueled by a true passion for Europe and for democracy, the voice from inside the deepest of all resistance movements against Hitler and fascism was the voice of *Count Richard N. Coudenhove-Kalergi* in his book *Paneuropa (1926)*.

The most interesting aspect of the book is the clear insight that a united Europe will, if ever, be brought about only through a gradual process of *integration*.[28] The author sees this gradual process realized through four consecutive steps:

- The creation of a pan-European conference;

- The conclusion of an obligatory arbitrage and guarantee agreement;

- A European customs unification for bringing about a European economic union;

- The realization of the *United States of Europe* after the example of the *United States of America* through a pan-European Constitution and a supranational parliament consisting of two houses: the Congress and the House of Representatives.[29]

In no previous plan for a European integration the various phases of a step-by-step building of the community were pointed out with that precision and clarity. In so far, the inte-

Published by Sirius-C Media Galaxy LLC, 2010

grational draft convention by Coudenhove-Kalergi can be seen as the antithesis to Rousseau's constitutional model.

In the years to come, the pan-European ideas were motivating and fueling the resistance movements not only against Hitler, but also against Mussolini in Italy and the Vichy regime in France. These peace plans, that were further elaborated in the anti-fascist underground between the two world wars were directly flowing into the European integration dynamism of post-World War II.[30]

Integration vs. Constitution

With the *European Community for Coal and Steal (Montan Union)* in 1951, the historical foundation was laid for the prototypical realization of a *European unification* in a relatively restricted, but economically important sector.[31]

The subsequent creation of the *European Economic Community (EEC)* in 1957 was a significant step ahead toward integration through the integrative vision of both the European Court of Justice and the European Parliament.[32]

It is interesting to note that the EEC was realized along the schema proposed by Coudenhove-Kalergi in that it came about through three essential unifications, first a governmental summit, second a contract followed by a trade union, followed, third, by the final step yet to be realized, the foundation of the political union that Coudenhove-Kalergi called 'The United States of Europe'.

The integration function of the *European Parliament* became especially important after the first direct election of the parliamentarians in 1979. This should however not let us forget that the most important lever for European integration is Article 18 EEC Charter that stipulates as the first integrative step the realization of a *trade union with a unified customs index* for all member states of the community.

The second fundamental integrative step then will be the *political union* or foundation of a European Republic through the unification of national political decision-making by the supranational decision-making of the *United States of Europe* that first of all would require a unified foreign politics.[33] This was the most important point in the proposal of the Belgian prime minister Leo Tindemans in 1975 which consolidated the results of the first official proclamation of the European Union during the Paris Summit in 1972.[34]

The Integrational Model

It is interesting to note that a unified foreign policy was namely not contained in the union's task catalog proposed by Tindemans, but that only a common attitude of all member states was required in this important point.[35] As the reader might remember from my discussion of the historical draft conventions, it is rather the constitutionalists such as Abbé de Saint-Pierre, Rousseau and Kant who require a *strong unified political force* and supranational executive power, whereas the integrationalists, Saint-Simon and Coudenhove-Kalergi, tend to be much more reluctant with conferring executive political powers to the unified political government of the new supra-national union.

And when we see that Tindemans was openly on the side of the integrationalists, we might better understand why his draft was lacking out in one of the most important constitu-ents of a true political union: a central government with in-dependent political powers and a strong executive.

In fact, Tindemans wrote the integrational system di-rectly in his report.[36] After the first direct election of the European Parliament, the *Genscher-Colombo-Plan* presented at the London Summit in 1981[37] represents a further milestone in the *integrative-pragmatic direction* and focuses on an extension of existing integrative levers, as for example a concerted action between the European Commission and the European Parliament and the revision of certain developments in the aftermath of the *Luxemburg Compromise* of 1966.[38]

A central point in this plan is the *European Political Cooperation (EPC)*[39] that was elaborated in the Luxembourg Rapport 1970, the Copenhagen Rapport 1973 and the London Rapport 1981.[40] The EPC, which was called in the London Rapport 1981 a *central factor of the member states' foreign policies*, is an obvious parallel to Abbé de Saint-Pierre's idea of a supranational governmental concertation, be it restricted to foreign policy. That the EPC can be developed into a true political union is subject to doubt, first because it has no normative function[41], and second because the important sector of a common defense policy for the European Union was from the start excluded.[42]

A political will to extend the range of what might be called high-level political partying is certainly not enough to bring about what is the most badly needed in present-day Europe: *a common defense strategy* and a concisely elaborated, unified foreign policy.

To repeat it, the invasion of Iraq showed where we are heading if Europe is *not to become a true political union* that forms an important democratic power block in 21st century world politics.

Published by Sirius-C Media Galaxy LLC, 2010

The Constitutional Model

Already during the foundation of the Montan Union, 1951-1952 there were negotiations for a later *European Defense Community (EDC)* and in that draft convention was foreseen that the Congress of that organization was given the competence for drafting a first *European Constitution*.

In an ad-hoc meeting a first draft for such a constitution was elaborated. However, as the EDC failed to be ratified by the French parliament, a unification of the national defense policies became obsolete.

A later attempt to unify national defense strategies contained in the so-called *Fouchet-Plans (1963)* failed as well, perhaps because of lacking vision regarding the need to elaborate a common defense policy.

But we still face a much more general question, which is, how to build a true *European Union* as a politically functional organism, and doing this without incorporating the unification of internal, external and defense politics? I think it must estrange any honest fighter for the European cause that unfortunately none of these crucial concerns was contained in the *Foundation of a European Union of February 14, 1984.*[43]

While in Part Four of the chart, an independent economic policy of the union is announced, none of the subsequent articles, especially Article 47, contains detailed provisions to this effect. What this draft thus represents is a *blank paper convention* with nothing to even slightly modify the status quo.

Instead of a common foreign policy, Article 64 enumerates as 'common action areas' only domains that anyway are within the competence of the EEC. Instead of a unified defense policy, Article 68 only contains a chewing-gum provision that says that 'the European Council can extent common action also for questions of foreign policy'.

Published by Sirius-C Media Galaxy LLC, 2010

A European Constitution?

We can thus conclude that historically two different models have been drafted that were elaborated for bringing about a European Union or European Republic, a *constitutional model* and an *integrational model*.

The *constitutional model* foresaw the creation of a *European Constitution* through some sort of concerted, unified and legislative action of the European sovereigns that resulted in a supranational government (Abbé de Saint-Pierre, Rousseau, Kant) or a *European Parliament* (Saint-Simon), conceding *independence and sovereignty* to this new organization in the general interest of all European member states and under the restriction of national interests.

The integrational model projects a federal Europe being brought about through a dynamic, phased process from a pan-European conference until the final step of a *pan-European republic*. This model, as I mentioned it already, was elaborated by Coudenhove-Kalergi, while the idea was already present with Saint-Simon.

In all peace proposals, a parliamentarian and republican political system was seen as an important 'in-group landmark' and condition for preparing the 'out-group achievement' of a supranational confederation in which all member states would *restrict their sovereignty* to a certain extent so as to grant independence and sovereignty to the new confederative legal and administrative body.

This idea is of such high impact that it goes like a red thread through all European politics until this very day. In fact, all present-day European integration projects are to be retraced to this tradition and historical parallel. European law experts agree about Article 237 of the EEC Charta containing an *unwritten condition* for the admission of new members: they must comply with the requirement of a *parliamentary democratic constitutional system* that however can also be formed as a constitutional monarchy.[44] As a matter of fact, Article 2 of the *Draft Convention of the European Parliament for a European Political Union* requires more than Article 237 of the EEC contract in that only a 'democratic European state' can apply for membership in the union.[45]

The discussion goes until our very days what the *precise requirements* are of that unwritten republican clause and they have been a part of the heated public debate about Turkey's anticipated membership.[46]

The details of this principle that it is valid as an unwritten addendum to Article 237 EEC contract are not controversial. As Nicolaysen pointed out:

Gert Nicolaysen

Doubts are not possible regarding the founding principles of the union's constitution: they can in Western Europe only be based upon democratic and civil rights; in addition, this constitution can in fact only be a republican one.[47]

When we look at the present-day attempts to bring about a European Union through drafting a *European Constitution*,

Published by Sirius-C Media Galaxy LLC, 2010

and compare these endeavors with the historical projects for bringing about peace and stability in Europe, we quickly recognize that we are looking in a simulation cabinet. What is presented with lots of pomp, glamour, power display and media coverage is in fact blindfolding the masses about a political reality in today's Europe I would qualify as 'stagnation' because the integrational dynamics appear to be regressing below a standard we have achieved about fifteen years ago.

I have tried to show that drafts and papers to bring about a true political union have deceived the public point by point since the *Luxemburg Compromise* of 1966 in that they did not contain one single of the founding constitutional elements we have seen present in all historical convention drafts.

To speak of a real European Union, simply because the original EEC now has not only six, but more than forty members, is another way to blindfold the media-hypnotized masses about the fact that surely in a sandbox of forty, litigations are going to be much more difficult, and not easier, to realize than in a sandbox of six. And to even dream of ideas being realized in a gigantic Europe of forty which were not realized in an initial Europe of six borders journalistic and political eye-wiping. From this perspective, it looks rather as Utopia than future reality to consider 'The United States of Europe' as a full political union being realized anywhere in the near future.

As a matter of fact, and as a bitter note to conclude this chapter, the only thing that was realized without problem for the greater Europe was the following:

▸ The creation of a supranational European police force called EUROPOL;

▸ Concerted action of all members to increasingly spy out and control citizens by lowering civil rights and constitutional guarantees;

▸ Concerted action of all members to create a common ID card for all European citizens that allows police and paramilitary forces to control and persecute individuals beyond national borders.

Nothing, by contrast, was foreseen and agreed upon that enlarges or safeguards civil rights and guarantees for new member states; the only advantages, then, it seems, for new members to join the union are of a mere financial nature.

No big deal after so much ado about nothing!

However, the European law expert will not for that matter give up being positive about a final success of the European unification idea; what was eye-wiping has been recognized as such; the intelligent, educated and critical European citizen intuitively knows that the media images cannot be trusted.

Beyond the perspective one can gain from politics, with all its absurdities, the expert knows that the real progress of the European idea was largely the long-term insistence upon *integration*, as an incremental and step-by-step process.

Personally, I am a believer in the *integration idea* because I have known the details and studied and practiced European law for a good time. My mistrust in the constitutionalist idea is because the door is wide open, with that kind of idea, for political cunningness, media manipulation and lobbyism un-

Published by Sirius-C Media Galaxy LLC, 2010

til outright media bluff. Nothing in our world that involves large masses of people and a change of the political landscape is created overnight, by publishing a decorated 'Constitution' that propagates the best for all, in no time, and for no price to pay, like the proverbial *manna* falling from heaven.

This is something good for the rainbow press, but not for those who, like myself, know the intricate details of the process. To say, the European idea is not dead, it's still very much alive, but it's better put in the hands of the generally invisible crowd of legal experts, advisors, administrators, and judges than in the white gloves of our glamorous politicians and their blind followers.

On the surface level, Europe 2012 will probably not be much different from Europe 2008, and for insiders and academia this is not something to regret. The transitions we are living through in this moment and over the next twenty years are of such a grandeur, of such a revolutionary impact, and of such a daringness that we cannot reasonably expect them to happen overnight, nor to be effected and carried out without hurt or sacrifices.

On the surface, changes seem to be nonexistent when in reality the time factor is such that slowness makes for steadiness; behind the veil of public appearance, where change is incremental and slow, true progress is being made.

This slowness of progress is not a bad thing to happen, by the way. All solid progress is slow, look only at plants, not to talk about the time from the big bang until today or the time our human race needed to emerge on the globe. When you look at a plant or a tree, you get the feeling that nothing is growing, or changing, and this is, as we all know, a wrong perception. When you see a tree that is a few hundred years old or a giant tortoise whose age can be up to three thousand years, you get an idea of the fact that time is relative and that for trees and giant tortoises, time is certainly different than for humans.

How can we predict how much time 'it should take' to transform a world of unfreedom, violence and rampant injustice into a world of freedom, of peace, of justice and of respect for all sentient beings? All religions have speculated about this important question, but at the end, when you have studied all this, and look at the present world, you become rather down-to-earth in your approach and you feel that such speculations really lead nowhere. What however contributes to change, and what progresses the change agenda, is positive thinking and consistency in upholding a vision and the values connected to it!

Many intelligent world citizens today have this vision and are lucidly aware of the necessary values behind this vision, and there is consensus about the core values of a functional and smooth society that is able to be of assistance to human progress, instead of opposing human progress. These values are obvious, they are so basic as values can be basic; we live in a world that is upside-down in every respect: there is war, strife, hunger, violence, and oppression, globally, and all this is not normal, and not in the genetic program of the human race.

To bring about peace, we need to focus on the *simple human values* that virtually every child knows and instinctively

Published by Sirius-C Media Galaxy LLC, 2010

follows, and which are love, respect, freedom, understanding of our needs, and help and support for those in growth, and those in need, and this without regard to race, ethnic belonging, culture, family background, or language.

All problems can be solved, provided there is a will, but this will is lacking in our present societies because the political priority is not problem-solving but *problem administration*.

There are many people, among them many politicians, who earn more money with *administrating our worldwide problems* than they would earn by solving them. Our endeavor for transforming present society is motivated and fueled by the idea of establishing a *world government* as the *safer solution* compared to a bunch of highly armed nation states who share in a scarcity paradigm, fighting for 'survival resources', thus jeopardizing world peace, and who, by their endless insistence on 'national values', in truth defy human values. The struggle for 'quick solutions' loses its attractiveness when you consider the bigger agenda and its ultimate purpose, *world peace*.

And applying the wisdom of the Book of Changes, the I Ching, we know that hastening growth regularly 'destroys the fruit'. Timeless wisdom and the observation of living systems coincide in affirming that every true and solid growth needs time, and that often, with larger projects, the time needed is very difficult to predict in advance.

The model, if ever, for building a united world, is not the United States but will be the *United States of Europe*, once they are realized. And this for very tangible reasons.

The United States of America, at the time of their creation were a *quite homogenous structure* compared to Europe, which is rather heterogenous. In addition, psychologically, the United States were *new land,* and the settlers were in quite the same situation, facing novelty, and thereby forming a common purpose, in alignment with their very similar needs and visions.

In Europe, every country has a different history and a still more strikingly different culture. To look at the three 'classical' examples, to show their essential difference in lifestyle, take Germany, France and Italy. Three countries, so different in cultural background, lifestyle and personal habits, so different in the culinary sector, so different in spending habits, so different in marriage and family attitudes and the education of children, and then you want to bring them under one hat, and let one government decide about their future?!

It's really an idea hostile to most European nationals, in their quality as nationals, in their role as Germans, French and Italians, while a lesser hostile idea in their role as Europeans. And it's exactly to what extent they accept their fresh 'European' identity that the whole idea is going to work, or is *not* going to work in the long run. And it's for that and other reasons that the testing arena for a possible world unification is not the USA but the USE, namely when we have mastered the challenge to get to look over our national fences, as these fences used to be high and opaque.

Published by Sirius-C Media Galaxy LLC, 2010

CHAPTER THREE

The Restriction of National Sovereignty

Introduction

In the present last chapter we are going to look at some examples and case law that demonstrate the fact that national sovereignty today is no more sacrosanct, as this was still the case before the 19th century.

Let me add here in a side note that *foreign sovereign immunity* should not be confounded with so-called state immunity, while in the literature the two terms are often used synonymously. But they are not synonymous. Sovereign immunity or state immunity regards the immunity of the national government vis-à-vis its own citizens, regularly in torts actions, when citizens have been harmed by civil servants, or by tax regulations or any coercive action done to the citizen by the state or federal authorities.

In such cases, the citizen can rightfully claim damages by suing their government in a torts action in front of an administrative court. Only in these cases, we speak of sovereign or state immunity.

The cases that I am going to reference hereafter in this chapter, however, involve *foreign* sovereign immunity, the immunity from jurisdiction or post-judgment attachment measures or the like, against a *foreign state*, in front of a tribunal of the nation, the forum state, the claimant is a citizen of. While both state immunity and foreign sovereign immunity are initially based upon the concept of *full national sovereignty*, they both have been severely restricted, if not eroded, which is a significant fact to note for the international law scholar in

Published by Sirius-C Media Galaxy LLC, 2010

that such a situation *signals a paradigm change of even wider dimensions in the future.* Why is that so? Let me explain, then. International law is widely built and developed by international practice, which is the way nation states behave on the international platform, both in bilateral and multilateral relationships.

What scholars and international law practitioners do, and also what judges do when they rule over questions that involve international law, is *not* lawmaking, it is a *not a normative behavior.* This is a very important fact to realize for the lay person, because otherwise the function of international law cannot be understood. The only 'persons' that are allowed to actually be *normative* in international law are the states themselves, the former sovereigns, the modern nation states, and their state departments. Their behavior then, is carefully observed and registered by international lawyers, scholars and other state departments, for how they move around in the world, what they do, what they don't do, what they want to do in the future, all this has *normative quality.* This is what actually forms and develops international law, it's called 'state practice', in a short term.

One may find that quite outlandish as an idea, but when you think about it, it's only logical. Where there is no international government, and accordingly, no international parliament, the norms and rules are set by the nations, simply because they have 'no superior'. That's why it's all so strange, it's also why it's all so interesting, so fascinating to study for a lawyer. It was for me, while I was never a passionate lawyer for domestic law, but European Law and International Law were for me as passionate topics to study as reading history novels or watch a reportage about the opium war.

Now, there is another subtle thing to note, that is the jurisprudence. We have an International Court of Justice in the Hague, Netherlands, but lay people often ignore that this court can rule only over conflicts resulting from international conventions *where the states member of that convention have expressly agreed to submit to the court any conflict arising from the treaty.* That is why the courts that rule over questions of foreign sovereign immunity are national courts, in the United States, the District Courts.

Now, the interesting thing is that those courts must be very qualified as their judges must do actually the same work as international law scholars, that is, law professors accredited at reputed universities, and for the US District Courts, I must say, they do this work admirably well! To repeat it, their judgments are *not normative* in the sense that their decisions would automatically form international law, while they are of course normative for the case pending at court; however, it is also true that when there is a *consistency of such jurisprudence over a considerable time*, and when such consistency covers not just one nation but the jurisprudence of a *number of nations*, agreeing thus on seeing certain things in a certain way, then we speak of a 'new rule in international law' that is built by state practice. The courts did not by themselves make the rule, but in that their decisions were so constant over time, one must conclude that a *consistent state practice can be made out that over a certain time formed that new rule in international law.*

Published by Sirius-C Media Galaxy LLC, 2010

State Trading and Sovereignty

An area where a clear restriction of national sovereignty was occurring is *international trade*, particularly with regard to commercial contracts where one party of the agreement is a private trader, and the other party, a foreign state.

While still two hundred years ago, governments hardly entered the marketplace for purchasing goods, and manufactured themselves all the goods and materials needed for their governmental purposes, this changed with the emergence of world trade during the 19th century. As a result, international law has widely changed from about the beginning of the 19th century. Against the opinion of many skeptical international law experts, international law has stood trial as to its ability to flexibly adapt to paradigm changes in socioeconomic conditions as well as to the psychology of nations' behavior on the international stage.

Are we dealing with a law of sovereigns, or with a law of nations? How did sovereigns behave in the past, and how do our modern nation states behave? When we look at these questions, we can observe a tremendous *shift in international jurisdiction* from about the last decade of the nineteenth century. This paradigm shift was subtly prepared by incidental precedents such as *The Schooner Exchange (1812)*[48] and culminated in a thorough reform of international procedural law. Let me explain.

Before the 19th century, sovereigns, or rulers, were considered immune from any jurisdiction other than their own.

This was historically and politically a sound concept until the moment when, from about the middle of the 19th century, the young nation states engaged in the growing international market and behaved, as such, like traders. In my doctoral thesis, I elucidated the procedural questions, the evidence problems and the burden of proof in such litigations against foreign states and their agencies and instrumentalities.[49]

The fact that the nation states entered the international marketplace for buying and selling goods set a novelty event on the timeline of human history. International law was not prepared to deal with that novelty at first, and could not protect private traders from losing huge sums of money because they had contracted with a foreign government; what namely happened quite regularly in these cases was that the foreign government would invoke 'foreign sovereign immunity' in order to escape its liability under the contract.

The consequence of the immunity claim was namely that the forum state had to deny jurisdiction over the foreign state, and dismiss the claim because of a 'procedural handicap'. When a claim is dismissed on procedural grounds, the court *will not enter the substance matter* of the case, and thus not rule over the transaction that was at the basis of the claim. The lawyer would in such a case reason their client that 'the case cannot be won because of lacking jurisdiction'.

Thus what the new situation created was *rampant injustice*, and heavy financial losses of large trading companies around the world as a result of having contracted not with a private trading company but with a foreign state, or an agency or instrumentality of a foreign state.

Published by Sirius-C Media Galaxy LLC, 2010

One can figure that in the beginning courts were reluctant to affirm jurisdiction over foreign states, while they were well aware of the blatant cynicism of the situation. The novelty was overwhelming and they found international law had no instrument to deal with the problem. And as the topic was a sensitive one because the principle of national sovereignty was in play, judges tended to be very careful. They did not want to step on the feet of some or the other foreign government, and still less did they want to offend their state department or department of foreign affairs.

Some however were conscious that a historical break was about to happen and that it was more or less blunt injustice done to the private claimants *to grant immunity to a state who voluntarily engaged in the market place* and then pleaded sovereign immunity as a defense in an action that did not concern sovereign but commercial activities of that state.

As the business volume of most of those cases was considerable, judges soon found a way to avoid such injustice. They argued that it was *not the nature of the person* involved, speak the private individual or sovereign ruler or state, that was decisive for the granting or not of immunity, but the *nature of the activity in question*.

That was after all a clever strategic move to go around the intricate sovereignty question. 'We are not going to touch the sovereignty of the state. We look what states are doing, and upon their acting they are judged, not upon their nature; their sovereignty thus remains untouched.'

The reasoning was brilliant and efforts of highly qualified international defense lawyers who worked pro immunitatem eventually failed. At that point, the law was changing, and nobody could prevent that tremendous paradigm shift from happening. International law was going to get a new face! It was almost a revolution, despite the fact that people other than government consultants and international lawyers had (and have) hardly an idea of these affairs, as they are not catchy topics for the international mass media.

The lawyers who worked on the side of the private merchants argued that if the activity in question was by its nature commercial, the state was to be denied immunity and the foreign court had to affirm jurisdiction. If, however, the act or activity was sovereign, then immunity had to be granted and jurisdiction was to be denied. That was indeed a handy rule that was quickly to become a sort of standard for judging sovereign immunity questions before national tribunals.

And the change of international law in this respect demonstrates that international law is well flexible and open to change, when change is needed to uphold justice and avoid flagrant injustice! International conferencing, while it's today a popular topic in the international media, is not the primary lever for change in matters of international law. International law changes rather incrementally, and this most of the time *through case law*. This is exactly what happened with the development of the *restrictive immunity concept*.

This concept evolved from the end of the 19th century until today, and this process is still ongoing, and all the details and modifications of this concept were worked out by case law in agreement with international law experts and scholars,

Published by Sirius-C Media Galaxy LLC, 2010

international lawyers and consultants, not, or only to a minor extent, by international agreements.

The Allocation of the Burden of Proof

One may imagine, even as a lay person, how important it is to know the allocation of the burden of proof in matters of sovereign immunity litigation, for it often is crucial for winning the case. If, for example, the plaintiff bears the full procedural and substantial burden of proving the essentials of his claim, as it is under general civil law, and common law, then the restrictive immunity theory would not have gained much value in practice, as in most cases foreign states could go away with dishonoring commercial agreements, thus causing immense financial losses to the private sector.

Accordingly, among the array of questions I was essentially discussing in my doctoral thesis, the problem who bears the *burden of proof* in litigations where foreign sovereign immunity is claimed, was by far the most important.

The question of the burden of proof is originally not a matter of international law, but of the applicable national substantive law.[50] Needless to add that a case must have the necessary minimal contacts so that a national tribunal can affirm jurisdiction.

While under the United States' *Foreign Sovereign Immunities Act of 1976*[51], this question is stuck together with the question of the burden of proof, as a matter of legislative wording, minimal contacts is quite a different problem.[52] The interesting question comes up if, as a result of a quite homogenous national range of immunity laws, *international law was formed in a way so as to encompass today an evidence rule in the field of sovereign immunity?* In my thesis, I came to an affirmative conclusion, and time has given me right, as now twenty-one years after my public thesis presentation, the *International Law Commission* has codified the matter along the lines of my thesis conclusions, in the *United Nations Convention on Jurisdictional Immunities of States and their Property (2004).*[53]

To begin with, let me present an example for the interplay between national substantive law and jurisdictional immunity, *as a matter of international law*, with respect to the burden of proof.

Lets suppose a private merchant claims damages for the repudiation of a contract signed with a foreign state. In such a case, there is today no question that the claimant bears the burden to proof as to the existence of the title, the contract. But who bears the burden of proof for the facts that determine the outcome of the question of sovereign immunity?

Obviously, it would be easy if the burden here would also be on the claimant. It would simplify the evidence procedure. Unfortunately, things are not that simple. Even though often the two burdens may coincide, this is not always so, especially not under the *Foreign Sovereign Immunities Act of 1976 (FSIA)* of the United States.

Theoretically, there are two options to design the burden of proof for substantiating the sovereign immunity claim:

> ▸ i) the burden is on the plaintiff for demonstrating the commercial character of the transaction;

▶ ii) the burden is on the foreign state to prove that the nature of the transaction was exceptionally governmental.

I shall in the following summarize the main results of my analysis, without being too explicit; in fact in my doctoral thesis and my recent monograph I have effected a detailed comparative law analysis of all six immunity statutes that at the time were prevalent for assessing the content of international law on the matter. Here only the general principle is of importance; when we see how, and how thoroughly, national sovereignty has been restricted, even if only in commercial matters, we see that the future is open for the creation of a world government.

The crucial condition for this to happen is lucid awareness of the *malignant cancer of national sovereignty,* a concept that hopefully will eventually be confined to safe boundaries.

A first and decisive step on this way were the following legal instruments, that were created between 1976 and 1982, and that are in my view important legal codifications regarding world democracy, in the true sense.

And interestingly so, once again the old insight was confirmed that commercial law and fair trade are the cornerstones for our world legal system to improve and evolve, because *trading is communication*, and as such it requires the *respect of human values* like free will, contractual freedom, *pacta sunt servanda* and legal predictability. In the absence of these values, no world trade is possible; without world trade to function smoothly, the mere *idea of world government* would appear grotesque and nonsensical. These statutes are:

Published by Sirius-C Media Galaxy LLC, 2010

▸ **The Foreign Sovereign Immunities Act, 1976**
(United States)

▸ **The State Immunity Act, 1978**
(United Kingdom)

▸ **The State Immunity Act, 1979**
(Singapore)

▸ **The State Immunity Ordinance, 1981**
(Pakistan)

▸ **The Foreign States Immunities Act 87, 1981**
(South Africa)

▸ **The State Immunity Act 1982**
(Canada)

My scrutiny and comparison of these different national statutes on foreign sovereign immunity revealed *common principles on the allocation of the burden of proof* with regard to both immunity from jurisdiction and immunity from execution.

Before going more in detail, let me shortly explain the difference between 'jurisdictional' and 'executional' immunities. It's in fact something so basic and common-sense that a lay reader can easily understand it. When you sue a foreign state in your national jurisdiction, and the state invokes the sovereign immunity claim, we are dealing with 'jurisdictional' immunity; if however you are a judgment creditor of that state, having already received a judgment against the foreign state that entitles you to receiving payment or indemnities, and you seek satisfaction, then we are dealing with 'executional' immunities. In addition, there is an important variation of the latter constellation; for example you have done repairs of a foreign state's embassy in your country, and they don't pay the bill after you finished the work. Even before having a judgment against them, you want to *secure your interests* by seizing, by act of law, one of the embassy's bank accounts for your satisfaction; in such a case we are equally dealing with 'executional' immunities.

Immunity from Jurisdiction

With regard to immunity from jurisdiction, the burden of proof is in principle on the foreign state to show some factual basis of its immunity claim by establishing a *prima facie case* of immunity. This means the state must provide some evidence, not a full proof, for the court to affirm immunity and deny jurisdiction. When forwarding evidence for establishing this prima face case, the foreign state is not obliged to disprove all immunity exceptions, but only the one(s) the plaintiff relies on. If the plaintiff does not specify exception(s) he relies on, the foreign state can generally affirm, by *affidavit*[54] or otherwise, that it falls under the range of the statute, and thus –

> ▸ that it is a foreign state within the definition of the statute, and

> ▸ that the act or activity in question was of a public, governmental nature.

Once the foreign state has made its case, the evidential burden shifts to the plaintiff to prove the applicability of the exception(s) he relies on. If the plaintiff fails to establish an exception to immunity, immunity has to be granted since the prima facie evidence provided by the foreign state erects a 'presumption of immunity'. If, on the other hand, the foreign state fails to show some prima facie basis of immunity, the ultimate burden or persuasive burden would be with the foreign state and immunity would have to be denied.

This is however only so if the plaintiff, in his pleadings, has given convincing proof for the court to qualify the activity in question as *commercial*. Since, in this case, no presumption has been erected, and international law does not contain any presumption in favor of immunity or in favor of jurisdiction, the court cannot, without endangering the sovereignty of the foreign state, deny immunity without further enquiry and only on the basis of the burden of proof. In this case, the court must namely qualify the activity in question *on the basis of all the evidence* the parties have submitted. The court is notably not allowed to refuse immunity only because the foreign state has not entered an appearance or otherwise failed to defend itself. The fact that the restrictive immunity doctrine imposes a certain rule of the burden of proof does not mean that the court is liberated from its obligation to rule *sua sponte (ex officio)* on the question of immunity.

The statutes slightly differ in the provisions concerning *agencies or instrumentalities* or *separate entities* of the foreign state.

Whereas the American and Canadian statutes assimilate agencies and instrumentalities, for jurisdictional immunity purposes, the British and related statutes split separate entities from the foreign state and erect a presumption of non-immunity to their effect.

Under the American and Canadian immunity statutes, the burden of proof, *without presumption,* is the same for agencies or instrumentalities of the foreign state. In practice the results of the two different approaches however hardly differ as to the burden of proof, for the foreign state must, in its prima facie evidence, join some proof that the agency or instrumentality in question belongs to the foreign state, rather than being an entity distinct from it.

It is logical that the privilege of sovereign immunity is not granted to legal entities distinct from foreign states. That is why, in practice, the American and Canadian statutes can also be said to contain *presumptions of non-immunity* with regard to such distinct legal entities, despite the fact that the text of these statutes, as to the burden of proof, is less clear than the other enactments on foreign sovereign immunity.

Immunity from Execution

With regard to immunity from execution, the old rule that is called *absolute rule of sovereign immunity* has not been altered. It stayed intact as a true general rule of sovereign immunity, despite the fact that the statutes concede some exceptions to this rule, notably the absence of immunity if the property in question was used, by the foreign state, for (exclusively) commercial purposes.

Since the rule of immunity from execution is not only a residual concept, as is the rule of immunity from jurisdiction, no prima facie evidence is necessary from the side of the foreign state to erect this immunity rule into a true presumption. Only the British, Pakistani and Singapore acts require to this effect a special ambassadorial certificate. But this requirement is no onus for foreign states and has not to fulfill the standards of a prima facie case. It is more of a formality, easily to be rendered by the head of the foreign state's embassy – a *simple statement* to the effect that the assets in question did not serve commercial purposes, but were used for the daily running of the embassy. Its effect is the erection of a presumption of immunity for the property in question.

The burden of proof for overcoming this presumption is squarely put in the lap of the judgment creditor, as it is the case under the statutes which do not contain such a certificate provision.

The normal evidence procedure, as the persuasive burden clearly remains with the judgment creditor, is such that the latter begins to present proof by submitting prima facie evidence that the property in question was used, by the foreign state, for commercial purposes. If the judgment creditor succeeds in establishing this *prima facie case*, the foreign state, by simply contradicting this proof, can be granted sovereign immunity, since the general rule of immunity from execution is on its side. Even if the foreign state is not able to contradict the prima facie evidence of the judgment creditor, the latter must prove, by a preponderance of the evidence, the applicability of an exception to immunity from execution. This is notably the consequence of ordinary rules of statutory construction that put the burden of proof on the one who struggles against a general rule contained in a statute. This burden is *not met by prima facie evidence*, but only by a plain proof overcoming the presumption established under the general rule.

Thus, the *immunity risk* in matters of immunity from execution is clearly on the judgment creditor. In other words, the judgment creditor bears the *legal or persuasive burden of proof.* In any case of doubt (non liquet), the court must grant immunity. In other words, in matters of immunity from execution, the rule is *in dubio contra immunitatem.*

For certain types of property (military property or property of a foreign central bank), the statutes tend to be even more severe. They only differ in either refusing any execution (thus granting absolute immunity in the true sense) or permitting a very limited range of executory measures.

The Signal Function of Restricted Sovereignty

We have seen in our detailed analysis of the *restrictive foreign sovereign immunity doctrine* that the transition from the paradigm of 'absolute' immunity to the new standard of 'restrictive' took more than a hundred years.

That seems to be a very long time but is compared to the whole of human history a tiny event on the timeline of human evolution. And while as such it may have interest only for specialized lawyers, the signal function of this restriction of national sovereignty cannot be underestimated.

Notably, in English, a *restriction* connotes something being 'restrained' in its scope, power or expression. We have seen that the once unlimited national sovereignty of a nation state today is restrained for the domain of jurisdictional immunities, when the activity in question was of a private, commercial nature.

When such a trend is to be traced, and corroborated by case law, and when the general idea has been accepted that sovereignty is *not per se an 'absolute' power,* but can well be restrained, and must be restrained when it brings harm to people, companies and to national economies, then we have a situation where, as lawyers say, a 'precedent was set'. When a precedent was set, there is a likelihood that a similar constellation or situation will be judged *along the same lines* because of the similarity of interests or because the values to be protected are of a similar nature.

Published by Sirius-C Media Galaxy LLC, 2010

On the same line of reasoning, the text of the *European Convention on State Immunity*, 1972, states in its Preamble, that it takes into account 'the fact that there is in international law a tendency to restrict the cases in which a State may claim immunity before foreign courts'.

The *United Nations Convention on Jurisdictional Immunities of States and their Property (2004)*, contains a similar clause. These clauses are of course very general and have a mere declaratory character, but they are nonetheless important because of their signal function.

We have to keep in mind that only a hundred years ago such a clause in an international treaty would have been unthinkable as such an international convention wouldn't have been agreed upon; the majority of states would have thought of such a clause as 'offending their sovereignty'. The concept of sovereignty has to be seen historically; the coming up of nation states was a Renaissance endeavor, and would again have been unthinkable during the Middle-Ages because of the Church's absolute power. But when the Church's power was restrained, the nation states took over the sacrosanct nature of the Church's absolute domain, and by creating the idea of 'national sovereignty' expressed their claim of almost divine 'untouchability', and a set of absolute powers connected with it.

This is actually a good example for showing how cyclic human history is, and how nonlinear. It is cyclic in the sense that the same problems are put on the same stage but in the *disguise of different actors*, until humanity has gained enough consciousness to tackle the problem itself, instead of addressing the actor that embodies it. Not the Church was bad but the concept of total dominion over subjects treated as vassals; not the nation states are bad but again the concept of absolute, and sacrosanct, *sovereignty* because it does harm to people, and to the smoothness of international trade, and the communication between peoples. Thus, we can say that humanity has recognized 'the problem' twice, first in identifying the human rights abuses committed by the Church, second by realizing that absolute sovereignty, to mention only the commercial sector, brings heavy losses to private traders and a possible scenario of 'total injustice' into international trade, which cannot reasonably be tolerated.

As the problem of national sovereignty is larger, and does harm also in other ways than commercially, especially when we think that it is the single most dangerous trigger for wars between nation states, resulting in *heavy loss of human life*, the signal function given from the commercial sector is not to be overlooked and needs to be carefully analyzed by international law scholars and world peace organizations!

For me, in my quality of an international lawyer, the slow but steady erosion of national sovereignty is a fact that cannot be overlooked. Currently, we are in a transition period until about the year 2020 during which the concept of national sovereignty *is going to do even more harm,* but also where human consciousness will considerably rise to acknowledging the perilous nature of the very construct of sovereignty. This, then, will open the door to a modification and further restriction of sovereignty in the sense of restraining it by multilateral agreement, and giving a large part of sovereign national

Published by Sirius-C Media Galaxy LLC, 2010

power over to a supranational body called 'world government' or otherwise.

Behold, this is *not a utopian idea* but already now a process and dynamics that cannot be overlooked! The fact that in the international media little is to be heard about it, has to do with the fact that the matter is politically sensitive because national pride, and a whole bunch of chauvinist values are connected and associated with it.

In sensible matters of this kind, international diplomacy has developed a careful approach of incremental and careful progress that doesn't offend the main sandbox players, as so doing would in the long run only result in regional and international setbacks.

BIBLIOGRAPHY

General Bibliography

A

Adede, A.D.

*The United Kingdom Abandons the Doctrine of
Absolute Sovereign Immunity*
6 BROOKLYN J. INT'L L. 1997-215 (1980)

Aguda, Akinola

Law and Practice Relating to Evidence in Nigeria
London: Sweet & Maxwell, 1980

American Law Institute

Model Code on Evidence
Chestnut, Philadelphia, 1942

Asencio, Diego C. & Dry, Robert W.

*An Assessment of the Service Provisions of the Foreign
Sovereign Immunities Act of 1976*
8 JOURNAL OF LEGISLATION (Notre Dame Law School) 230-249 (1981)

Ashman, Allan

People's Republic Told to Pay $42.1 Million Debt From 1911
Jackson v. People's Republic of China
69 A.B.A.J. 512(2) (1983)

Augenti

L'onere della prova
Roma, 1932

Australia

The Law Reform Commission
Reform of Evidence Law 1980
Discussion Paper N° 16
Canberra: Australian Government Publishing Service, 1980

B

Badr, Gamal Moursi

State Immunity
An Analytical and Prognostic View
The Hague: Martinus Nijhoff, 1984

Bankas, Ernest K.

The State Immunity Controversy in International Law
Private Suits Against Sovereign States
New York: Springer, 2005

Barnes, A. James, Dworkin, Terry and Richards Eric L.

Law for Business, 9th Edition
New York: McGraw-Hill, 2006

Bartholomew, G.M.

The Commercial Law of Malaysia
A Study in the Reception of English Law
Singapore: Malayan Law Journal Ltd., 1965

Bennion, Francis

Statutory Interpretation
London: Butterworths, 1984

Published by Sirius-C Media Galaxy LLC, 2010

Berber, Friedrich

Lehrbuch des Völkerrechts
München: Beck, 1977
Erstmals veröffentlicht im Jahre 1969

Beutler/Bieber/Pipkorn/Streil

Die Europäische Gemeinschaft
Rechtsordnung und Politik
2. Auflage
Baden-Baden: Nomos, 1982

Bird S.

The State Immunity Act of 1978
13 INT'L LAWYER 619-643 (1979)

Block, Mark A.

De Sanchez v. Banco Central de Nicaragua:
An Extension of the Restrictive Theory of Sovereign Immunity
7 N.C.J.INT'L L. & COMM.REG. 419-431 (1982)

Brownlie, Ian

Principles of Public International Law
Oxford: Clarendon Press, 1966

Bodin, Jean

On Sovereignty (1576)
Six Books of the Commonwealth
Edited by Professor Julian Franklin
New York: Seven Treasures Publications, 2009

Bowett, D.W.

The State Immunity Act 1978
37 Cambridge L.J. 193-196 (1978)

Bowman & Harris

Multilateral Treaties
Index and Current Status
London: Butterworths, 1984

Botha, Neville

Some Comments on the Foreign States immunities Act 87 of 1981
XV COMP. & INT'L L.J. SOUTH AFRICA 334-343 (1982)

Bradley, A.G.

Service of Process under the Foreign Sovereign Immunities Act of 1976:
The Arguments For Exclusivity
14 CORNELL INT'L L.J. 357-368 (1981)

Brittenham, David L.

Foreign Sovereign Immunity and Commercial Activity: A Conflicts Approach
83 COLUM.L.REV. 1440-1512 (1983)

Brocá/Majada

Práctica Procesal Civil
Tome I
Barcelona: Bosch, 1979

Brooke, Julia

The International Law Association Draft Convention on Foreign Sovereign
Immunity:
A Comparative Approach
23 VA.J.INT'L L. 635 (1983)

Brower/Bistline/Loomis

The Foreign Sovereign Immunities Act of 1976 in Practice
73 AJIL 200 (1979)

Published by Sirius-C Media Galaxy LLC, 2010

Brownlie, Jan

Principles of Public International Law
Oxford: Clarendon Press, 1976

Butler, W. E.

International Law in Comparative Perspective
Ed. By William Elliott Butler
Alphen an den Rijn: Sijthoff en Noordhoff, 1980

Comparative Approaches to International Law
190 RCADI (1985-I), 9-90

C

Cairns, Bernard C.

Australian Civil Procedure
Sydney: The Law Book Company Ltd., 1981

Cairns, G.

Jurisdiction: Foreign Sovereign Immunities Act
TEX.INT'L L.J. 277-289 (1981)

Canada

Uniform Evidence Act, Livre II
Règles Générales de Preuve, Titre I, Fardeau de la Preuve

Commission de Réforme du Droit du Canada
Rapport sur la Preuve (Premier Rapport)
Ottawa: Ministre des Approvisionnements et Services, 1977

Report of the Federal/Provincial Task Force on Uniform Rules of Evidence
Prepared for the Uniform Law Conference of Canada
Toronto: The Carswell Company Ltd., 1982 [U.L.C.C. Report]

Cappelletti, Mauro & Perillo, Joseph M.

Civil Procedure in Italy
The Hague: Martinus Nijhoff, 1965

Carl, B.M.

Suing Foreign Governments in American Courts:
The United States Foreign Sovereign Immunities Act in Practice
33 SOUTHWESTERN L.J. 1009-1077 (1979)

Castel, Jean-Gabriel

Droit International Privé Québécois
Toronto: Butterworths, 1980

Canadian Conflict of Laws
2nd Edition
Toronto: Butterworths, 1986

Charlesworth & Percy

On Negligence
7th Edition
London: Sweet & Maxwell, 1983

Coad, Brian Douglas

The Canadian State Immunity Act
XIV LAW & POL'Y INT'L BUS. 1197-1220 (1982-83)

Crocker, Lawrence

Sovereign Immunity in the United States
29 I.C.L.Q. 580-510 (1980)

Chia, J.

Reception of English Law under Section 3 and 5 of the Civil Law Act 1956
Revised 1972
1974 J.MALAYAN COMM.L. 42

Published by Sirius-C Media Galaxy LLC, 2010

Clerk & Lindsell

On Torts
15th Edition
London: Sweet & Maxwell, 1982

Coester-Waltjen, Dagmar

Internationales Beweisrecht
Ebelsbach am Main: Gremer, 1983 (Münchner Universitätsschriften, Juristische Fakultät, Band 53)

Coudenhove-Kalergi, Richard N.

Paneuropa
Wien-Leipzig: Paneuropa Verlag, 1926

Couture, Eduardo J.

Fundamentos del Derecho Procesal Civil
Buenos Aires: Depalma, 1981

Coyne, Thomas A.

Rules of Civil Procedure for the United States District Courts
Practice Comments
New York: Clark Boardman Company Ltd., 1983

Cross, Sir Rupert

Cross on Evidence
5th ed.
London: Butterworths, 1979

Cross on Evidence
2nd Australian Edition
By J.A. Gobbo, David Byrne, J.D. Heydon
Sidney: Butterworths, 1980

Cross, Sir Rupert & Wilkins, Nancy

An Outline of the Law of Evidence
5th Edition
London: Butterworths, 1980

Curzon, L.B.

Law of Evidence
Plymouth: McDonald & Evans Ltd., 1978

D

Dalai Lama

Ethics for the New Millennium
New York: Penguin Putnam, 1999

Dalloz

Encyclopédie Juridique
2e Édition, Procédure III, 'Preuve'

David, René

Les Grands Systèmes de Droit Contemporains
6e Édition
Paris: Dalloz, 1974

English Law and French Law
London: Steven & Sons, 1980

Davis, A. J.

Sexual Assaults in the Philadelphia Prison System and Sheriff's Van
Trans-Action 6, 2, 8-16 (1968)

Published by Sirius-C Media Galaxy LLC, 2010

D, Carl IV

The Foreign Sovereign Immunities Act of 1976
N.C.J.INT'L L. & COMM.REG. 206-233 (1978)

Dean & Bruyn-Kops

The Crime and the Consequences of Rape
New York: Thomas, 1982

Delaume, Georges R.

The State Immunity Act of the United Kingdom
73 AJIL 185-199 (1979)

Transnational Contracts
Applicable Law and Settlement of Disputes
(A Study in Conflict Avoidance)
New York, Oceana

Ducharme, Léo

Précis de la Preuve
En matière civiles et commerciales
2e Édition
Ottawa: Éditions de l'Université d'Ottawa, 1982

Dubey, Harihar Prasad

The Judicial Systems of India
Bombay: N.M. Tripathi Private Ltd., 1968

Dugard, John

International Law in South Africa:
The Restrictive Approach to Sovereign Immunity Approved
1980 SOUTH AFRICAN L.J. 317

Dutoit, Bernard

Droit comparé et droit international public
Paris, 1976

E

Echandia, Hernando Davis

Teoría General de la Prueba Judicial
Tomo I, 5e Ed.
Buenos Aires: Victor P. De Zavalia, 1981

Eder, Phanor J.

A Comparative Study of Anglo-American and Latin American Law
New York: New York University Press, 1950

Eggleston, Sir Richard

Evidence, Proof and Probability
2nd Edition
London: Weidenfels & Nicholson, 1983

Eisner, Frédéric W.

*Beweislastfragen und Beweiswürdigung im deutschen
und amerikanischen Zivilprozess*
ZZP, Bd. 89, 78-90

Enriquez, Emilio Rioseco

La prueba ante la Jurisprudencia
Derecho Civil y Procesal Civil, Parte General y Reglas Comunes
Secunda Edición
Santiago: Editorial Jurídica de Chile, 1982

Published by Sirius-C Media Galaxy LLC, 2010

Erasmus, Gerhard

Proceedings against Foreign States
– the South African Foreign States Immunities Act
SOUTH AFRICAN Y.B.INT'L L. 92-105 (1982)

F

Fasching, Hans W.

Lehrbuch des österreichischen Zivilprozessrechts
Wien: Manz, 1984

Finkelhor, David

Sexually Victimized Children
New York: Free Press, 1981

Folz, Hans-Ernst

Die Geltungskraft fremder Hoheitsäusserungen
Eine Untersuchung über die anglo-amerikanische Act of State Doctrine
Baden Baden: Nomos, 1975

Fox, Hazel

The Law of State Immunity
Oxford: Oxford Library of International Law, 2004

G

García, Carlos A.

Derecho Procesal Civil
Mexico: Editorial Porrúa S.A., 1981

Ghestin, Jacques & Goubeaux, Gilles

Traité du Droit Civil
2e Édition
Paris: L.G.D.J., 1982

Glasbeek, Harry J.

Evidence Cases and Materials
Toronto: Butterworths, 1977

Cases and Materials on Evidence
Australian Edition
Sydney: Butterworths, 1974

Graham, Michael H.

Evidence
Text, Rules, Illustrations and Problems
The Commentary Method
St. Paul (Minn.): National Institute for Trial Advocacy, 1983

Federal Rules of Evidence in a Nutshell
St. Paul (Minn.): American Textbook Series, 1981

Grzybowsky, Kazimierz

Soviet Public International Law, Doctrines - Diplomatic Practice
Leyden: A.W. Sijthoff, 1970

Groeben/Boeckh/Thiesing/Ehlermann

Kommentar zum EWG-Vertrag
Band 2, Dritte Auflage
Baden-Baden: Nomos, 1983

Guggenheim, Paul

Traité de droit international public
Genève: Librairie de l'Université, 1967

Published by Sirius-C Media Galaxy LLC, 2010

Guldener, Max

Schweizerisches Zivilprozessrecht
3. Auflage
Zürich: Schulthess, 1979

H

Habscheid, Walther J.

Droit Judiciaire Privé Suisse
2e Édition
Genève: Librairie de l'Université, 1981

Habscheid, Walther J. & Schaumann, Wilfried

Die Immunität ausländischer Staaten nach Völkerrecht
und deutschem Zivilprozessrecht
Berichte der deutschen Gesellschaft für Völkerrecht (BDGVR), Bd. 8
Karlsruhe: C.F. Müller, 1968

Halsbury's Laws of England

4th Edition, Vol. 17, 'Evidence'
London: Butterworths

Halsbury's Statutes of England

3rd Edition, Vol. 48 (Continuation Volume)
London: Butterworths

Hansard Parliamentary Debates

5th Series, House of Lords, Official Report
Session 1977-1978
London: Butterworths

5th Series, House of Commons, Official Report
Session 1977-1978
London: Butterworths

Harvard Draft Convention

Competence of Courts in Regard to Foreign States
Rep. by Philip C. Jessup
26 AJIL 452 (1932 Suppl.)

Harvard University

A Uniform System of Citation
13th Edition
Cambridge, Mass.: Harvard Law Review Association, 1982

Hearing before the Subcommittee on Administrative Practice and Procedure

Committee of the Judiciary, United States Senate, 91st Cong.,
2nd Session, June 3, 1970
Washington, D.C., 1970

Henkin/Pugh/Schachter/Smit

International Law
Cases and Materials
St. Paul (West): American Casebook Series, 1980

Herman, Dean M.

A Statutory Proposal to Prohibit the Infliction of Violence upon Children
19 FAMILY LAW QUARTERLY, 1986, 1-52

Higgins, Rosalyn

Certain Unresolved Aspects of the Law of State Immunity
XXIX NETH.INT'L L.REV. 265 (1982)

Hilf, Meinhard

Die rechtliche Bedeutung des Verfassungsprinzips der parlamentarischen
Demokratie für den europäischen Integrationsprozess
Europa Recht 1984, pp. 9 ff.

Published by Sirius-C Media Galaxy LLC, 2010

Hoffmann & Zeffert

South African Law of Evidence
3rd Edition
Durban: Butterworths, 1983

Hobbes, Thomas

Leviathan (1651)
New York: Longman Library, 2006

House Report

H.R. Report 94-1487
15 ILM 1398 (1976), U.S.Code & Adm. News 6604 (1976)

Hunt Holmes, Patricia

*Establishing Jurisdiction under the Commercial-Activities Exception to the
Foreign Sovereign Immunities Act of 1976*
19 HOUS.L.REV. 1003-1023 (1982)

I

**Inter-American Draft Convention on Jurisdictional Immunity of
States**

22 ILM 292 (1983)

International Law Association (ILA)

Report of the Fifty-Ninth Conference Held at Belgrade, 1980

International Law Commission (ILC)

*United Nations Convention on Jurisdictional Immunities of States
and Their Property
Adopted by the General Assembly of the United Nations
on 2 December 2004*
Not yet in force. See General Assembly resolution 59/38, annex, Official

Records of the General Assembly, Fifty-ninth Session,
Supplement No. 49 (A/59/49)

J

James, Fleming & Hazard, Geoffrey

Civil Procedure
2nd Edition
Toronto: Little, Brown & Company, 1977

Johnson, Eric & Worthington, Chr.

Minimum Contacts Jurisdiction under the Foreign Sovereign Immunities Act
12 GA.J.INT'L & COMP.L. 209-230 (1982)

Jowitt's Dictionary of English Law

2nd Edition, by John Burke
London: Sweet & Maxwell, 1977

Jurisdiction of U.S. Courts in Suits Against Foreign States

U.S. Congress, House of Representatives
Subcommittee on Administrative Law and Governmental Relations
of the Committee on the Judiciary
Hearing, June 4, 1976
Washington, D.C., 1976

K

Kahale III, G. & Vega, M. A.

Immunity and Jurisdiction
Toward a Uniform Body of Law in Actions Against Foreign States
19 COLUM.J.TRANSNAT'L L. 211-258 (1979)

Published by Sirius-C Media Galaxy LLC, 2010

Kane
Suing Foreign Governments: A Procedural Compass
34 STAN.L.REV. 385 (1982)

Kélada, Henri

Code de Procédure Civile du Québec
Textes et Arrêts (Articles 1 à 481)
Montréal: Wilson et Lafleur Ltée, 1980

Kummer, Max

Grundriss des Zivilprozessrechts
3. Auflage
Bern: Stümpfli, 1978

L

Lal, Jadgish

Code of Civil Procedure, 1908
As amended up to date by C.P.C. Amendment Act N° 104 of 1976
Allahabad: Law Publishers Sardar Patel, 1981

Lalive, Jean-Flavien

Contrats entre États ou entreprises étatiques et personnes privées
181 RCADI (1983-III), pp. 13 ff.

L'immunité de juridiction des états et des organisations internationales
84 RCADI (1953-III), pp. 209 ff.

Lauterpacht, E., Q.C.

International Law Reports
Cambridge: Grotius Publishers

Lauterpacht, Hersch

International Law
Ed. By E. Lauterpacht, Q.C.
Vol. 3
London: Cambridge University Press, 1977

The Problem of Jurisdictional Immunities of Foreign States
28 BRIT.Y.B.INT'L L. 220-272 (1951)

Lehr, Ernest

Éléments de Droit Civil Anglais
2e Édition, par Jacques Dumas
Tome Premier
Paris: Sirey, 1906

Leigh, Monroe

Alberti v. Empresa Nicaraguense de la Carne (Case Note)
77 AJIL 888 (1983)

Jackson v. People's Republic of China (Case Note)
Foreign Sovereign Immunities Act – Liability of People's Republic
of China for defaulted 1911 bonds – state succession
77 AJIL 146-148 (1983)

Matter of Sedco, Inc. (Case Note)
Sovereign Immunity - Foreign Sovereign Immunities Act
Commercial Activity and Tortious Conduct Exception not Applicable
to Support Jurisdiction over Defendant in Oil Spill Disaster
77 AJIL 149-151 (1983)

Lilly, Graham C.

An Introduction to the Law of Evidence
St. Paul (West), 1978

Published by Sirius-C Media Galaxy LLC, 2010

Lipgens, Walter

Europa-Föderationspläne der Widerstandsbewegungen 1940-1945
München, 1968

Lugo, Andrea

Manuale di Diritto Processuale Civile
8e Ed.
Milano: A. Giuffrè, 1983

M

Machiavelli, Niccolo

The Prince
New York: Soho Books, 2009
Written in 1513
First posthumous publishing 1531

Der Fürst
Frankfurt/M: Insel Verlag, 2009

Mandrioli, Crisanto

Corso di Diritto Processuale Civile
Tome II: Il Processo di Cognizione
2e Ed.
Torino: G. Giappichelli, 1978

Mann, Francis A.

A New Aspect of the Restrictive Theory of Sovereign Immunity
31 I.C.L.Q. 573-575 (1982)

The State Immunity Act 1978
50 BRIT.Y.B.INT'L L. 43 (1979)

Materials on Jurisdictional Immunities of States and their Property

UN-Doc. ST/LEG- /SER.B./20
New York: United Nations, 1982

Maxwell on the Interpretation of Statutes

12th ed., by P. St. J. Langan
London: Sweet & Maxwell, 1969

Mazeaud

Leçons de Droit Civil
7e Édition, par François Chabas et Michel de Jughart
Paris: Éditions Montchrestien, 1983

McCormick

McCormick on Evidence
by Edward W. Cleary, 3d ed.
Lawyers Edition (Homebook Series)
St. Paul: West, 1984

McDougal/Reisman

International Law in Contemporary Perspective
The Public Order of the World Comity
Cases and Materials
New York: Foundation Press, 1981

McLeod, James G.

The Conflict of Laws
Calgary, Alberta: Carswell Legal Publishers, 1983

Merle, Roger & Vitu, André

Traité de Croit Criminel
Droit Pénal Spécial
Vol. II, par André Vitu
Paris: Editions Cujas, 1982

Published by Sirius-C Media Galaxy LLC, 2010

Micheli

L'onere della prova
Padova, 1942

Moore, James W.

Moore's Federal Practice
2nd Edition, 1979

Musielak, Hans Joachim

Die Grundfragen der Beweislast im Zivilprozess
Berlin, New York: De Gruyter, 1975

Musielak/Stadler

Grundfragen des Beweisrechts
München: Beck, 1984

N

Nagel, Heinrich

Internationales Zivilprozessrecht für deutsche Praktiker
Münster: Aschendorff, 1980

Nash, Gerard

Civil Procedure
Cases and Text
Sydney: The Law Book Company Ltd., 1976

Nash, Marian Lloyd

Digest of United States Practice in International Law
Vol. 1978
Washington, D.C.: Depart of State Publications 9162, 1980

Ninth Decennial Digest

American Digest System
Part I, 1976-1981

O

Oppenheim, Lassa

International Law
8th Edition, by Hersch Lauterpacht
New York, 1955
Originally published in 1905/1906

Organization of American States (OAS)

Inter-American Draft Convention on Jurisdictional Immunity of States
22 ILM 292 (1983)

P

Partsch, Karl Joseph

Die Anwendung des Völkerrechts im innerstaatlichen Recht.
Eine Überprüfung der Transformationslehre
Karlsruhe: C.F. Müller, 1964 (BDGVR, Bd. 6)

Patrikis, Ernest T.

Foreign Central Bank Property
Immunity from Attachment in the United States
1982 U.ILL.L.REV. 265-287

Pell, Terence J.

The Foreign Sovereign Immunities Act of 1976:
Direct Effects and Minimal Contacts
14 CORNELL INT'L.L.J. 97-115 (1981)

Published by Sirius-C Media Galaxy LLC, 2010

Phipson

Phipson on Evidence
13th ed., by John Huxley Buzzard
Richard May and M. N. Howard
London: Sweet & Maxwell, 1982

Phipson and Elliott

Manual of the Law of Evidence
11th Edition
by D. W. Elliott
London: Sweet & Maxwell, 1980

Pope, Russell J.

*Maritime Arrest Under the Foreign Sovereign Immunities Act:
An Anachronism*
62 TEX.L.REV. 511-535 (1983)

Prieto-Castro y Ferrándiz

Tratado de Derecho Procesal Civil
Pamplona: Editorial Aranzadi, 1982

Prütting, Hans

Gegenwartsprobleme der Beweislast
5. Auflage
München, Beck, 1965

R

Rapports Explicatifs Concernant la Convention Européenne

sur l'Immunité des États et le Protocole Additionnel
Strasbourg: Conseil de l'Europe, 1972

Raynaud, Pierre & Vanel, Marguerite

Répertoire de Procédure Civile
Paris: Éditions Montchrestien, 1984

Ress, Georg

Entwicklungstendenzen der Immunität ausländischer Staaten
40 ZaöRV 217 (1980)

Les tendances de l'évolution de l'immunité de l'État étranger
in: Droit international et droit interne
Édité par Michael Bothe et Raul E. Vinesa
Colloque argentino-allemand de droit constitutionnel,
Buenos Aires, 1979
Berlin: Duncker & Humblot, 1982 (Schriften zum Völkerrecht, Bd. 73)

Rigaldies/Turp/Woehrling

Droit International Public
Notes et Documents
Tome 3, Supplément
Montréal: Les Éditions Thémis, 1983

Rodriguez, Gustavo H.

Curso de Derecho Probatoria
4e Ed.
Bogotá: Ediciones Librería del Profesional, 1983

Rosenberg, Leo

Die Beweislast
5. Auflage
München und Berlin: Beck, 1965

Rosenberg/Schwab

Zivilprozessrecht
13. Auflage
München: Beck, 1981

Published by Sirius-C Media Galaxy LLC, 2010

Rothstein, Paul F.

Evidence in a Nutshell: State and Federal Rules
2nd Edition
St. Paul (West), 1981

Rousseau, Charles

Droit international public
Tome IV: Les relations internationales
Paris: Sirey, 1979

Row, Sanjiva

Code of Civil Procedure (Act V of 1908)
by Malik
3rd Edition, Vol. 1
Allahabad: Law Book Company, 1962

Rules of Civil Procedure for the United States District Courts

Practice Comments by Thomas A. Coyne
New York: Clark Boardman Company Ltd., 1983

S

Saint-Simon, Claude-Henri de

De la réorganisation de la société européenne
Avec Auguste Thierry
Paris, 1814
Lausanne: Centre de Recherches Européennes, 1967

Salmand & Heuston

On the Law of Torts
18th Edition
by R. F. V. Heuston and R. S. Chambers
London: Sweet & Maxwell, 1981

Sarkar's Law of Evidence

India, Pakistan, Bangladesh, Burma & Ceylon
13th Edition
by Prabhas C. Sarkar and Sudipto Sarkar
Calcutta: S. C. Sarkar & Sons, 1981

Sarkar on Civil Procedure

6th Edition, as amended by Act 104 of 1976
by Prabhas C. Sarkar and Sudipto Sarkar
Calcutta: S. C. Sarkar & Sons, 1979

Scardaccione, Aurelio

Le Prove
2d Ed.
Torino, 1971

Schmitthoff, C. M. & Wooldridge, F.

*The nineteenth century doctrine of sovereign immunity
and the importance of the growth of state trading*
2 DEN.J.INT'L L. & POL'Y 199 (1972)

Schubert, M. H.

*Federal Question Jurisdiction Over Actions Brought by
Aliens against Foreign States*
CORNELL INT'L L.J. 463-488 (1982)

Schwarzenberger, Georg

The Inductive Approach to International Law
London, 1965

Schwering, Walter

System der Beweislast im englisch-amerikanischen Zivilprozess
Karlsruhe: C. F. Müller, 1969 (Berkeley-Kölner Rechtsstudien, Bd. 11)

Published by Sirius-C Media Galaxy LLC, 2010

Sgro, Jill A.

China's stance on sovereign immunity: a critical perspective on Jackson v. People's Republic of China
22 COLUM.J.TRANSNAT'L L. 101-133 (1983)

Sheridan, C. A. (ed.)

Malaya and Singapore, The Development of their Laws and Constitutions
London: Steven & Sons, 1961

Siewert, Clark C.

Reciprocal Influence of British and United States Law:
Foreign Sovereign Immunity Law from the Schooner Exchange
to the State Immunity Act 1978
13 VAND.J.TRANSNAT'L L. 761-794 (1980)

Simmons, Kevin P.

The Foreign Sovereign Immunities Act of 1976:
Giving the Plaintiff His Day in Court
64 FORDHAM L.REV. 543 (1977)

Sinclair, Ian

The Law of Sovereign Immunity. Recent Developments.
167 RCADI (1980-II) 117

Singapore

Parliamentary Debates
Official Report, Vol. 39, 1979-80
The Laws of the Colony of Singapore, Edition of 1955

Sinnadurai, Visu

The Law of Contract in Malaysia and Singapore
Cases and Commentary
Kuala Lumpur: Oxford University Press, 1979

Smallwood, J. M.

*Recent Developments in the Anglo-American Doctrine of
Foreign Sovereign Immunity*
5 INT'L TRADE L.J. 296-318 (1980)

Smit, Hans

The Terms Jurisdiction and Competence in Comparative Law
10 AM.J.COMP.L. 164-169 (1961)

Smith, P. F. / Bailey, S.

The Modern English Legal System
London: Sweet & Maxwell, 1984

Steiner/Vagts

Transnational Legal Problems
Materials and Text
2nd Ed.
Minneola, N.Y.: Foundation Press, 1976

1982 Case and Documentary Supplement
Minneola, N.Y.: Foundation Press, 1982

Stern

Foreign Law in the Courts
Judicial Notice and Proof
54 Calif.L.Rev., 23 (1957)

Stone's Justices Manual

113th Edition
Ed. by John Richman and A. T. Draycott
London: Butterworths, 1981

Published by Sirius-C Media Galaxy LLC, 2010

Sucharitkul, Sompong

Developments and Prospects of the Doctrine of State Immunity
Some Aspects of Codification and Progressive Development
XXIX NETH.INT'L L.REV. 252 (1982)

Immunités Juridictionnelles des États et de leurs Biens
Rapports du rapporteur spécial
Annuaire de la Commission du Droit International, 1986,
Volume II, 2e Partie,
New York: Nations Unies, 1988
Annuaire de la Commission du Droit International, 1984,
Volume II, 2e Partie,
New York: Nations Unies, 1986

Immunities of Foreign States Before National Authorities
149 RCADI (1976-I) 86

State Immunities and Trading Activities in International Law
London: Steven & Sons, 1959

Sutherland

Statutory Construction
Ed. By Sands
4th Edition
London, 1975

Sutherland, P.

Recent Statutory Developments in the Law of Foreign Sovereign Immunity
7 AUSTRALIAN Y.B.INT'L L. 27-71 (1981)

Sweeny/Oliver/Leech

The International Legal System
Cases and Materials
2nd Edition
Minneola, N.Y.: Foundation Press, 1981

T

Tayer, James Bradley

A Preliminary Treatise on Evidence
1898

Tesón, Fernando A.

The Relations Between International Law and Municipal Law:
The Monism/Dualism Controversy
in: *International Law and Municipal Law,* ed. by Michael Bothe and
Raul E. Vinesa
Colloque argentino-allemand de droit constitutionnel
Buenos Aires, 1979
Berlin: Duncker & Humblot, 1982
(Schriften zum Völkerrecht, Bd. 73)

The English and Empire Digest

Vol. 22, 'Evidence'
London: Butterworths, 1974

The Pakistan Code

Vol. V (1880-1910)
Government of Pakistan
Karachi, 1966

The Statesman Yearbook

119th Edition, 1982-83
Ed. by John Paxton
London, 1982

Toffler, Alvin
Powershift
Knowledge, Wealth, and Violence at the Edge of the 21st Century
New York: Bantam, 1991

Published by Sirius-C Media Galaxy LLC, 2010

Revolutionary Wealth
How it will be created and how it will change our lives
New York: Broadway Business, 2007

The Third Wave
New York: Bantam, 1984

Troya Cevallos, José Alfonso

Elementos de Derecho Procesal Civil, Tomo 1
Quito: Centro de Publicaciones Pontificia Universidad
Católica del Ecuador, 1978

U

United Nations

Materials on Jurisdictional Immunities of States and their Property
UN-DOC. ST/LEG/SER.B./20
New York: United Nations, 1982 (UN-MAT.)

*United Nations Convention on Jurisdictional Immunities of States
and Their Property*
Adopted by the General Assembly of the United Nations
on 2 December 2004
Not yet in force. See General Assembly resolution 59/38, annex,
Official Records of the General Assembly
Fifty-ninth Session, Supplement No. 49 (A/59/49)

Urteaga, Pedro S.

Derecho Procesal Civil
Tomo II
Secunda Edición
Lima, 1982

V

Vallée, Charles

A propos de la convention européenne sur l'immunité des États
9 REV.TRIM.DR.EUR. 205 (1973)

Varela/Bezerra/Sampio e Nova

Manual de Processo Civil
Coimbra: Coimbra Editora Limitada, 1984

Von Mehren, R. B.

The Foreign Sovereign Immunities Act of 1976
17 COLUM.J.TRANSNAT'L L. 33-66 (1978)

W

Walder-Bohner, Hans Ulrich

Zivilprozessrecht
3. Auflage
Zürich: Schulthess, 1983

Walker & Walker

The English Legal System
6th Edition, by R.J. Walker
London: Butterworths, 1985

Walter, Pierre F.

Gibt es eine Beweislastverteilung bei der Immunität von Staaten?
30 RECHT DER INTERNATIONALEN WIRTSCHAFT (RIW/AWD) 9-14 (1984)

Evidence and Burden of Proof in Foreign Sovereign Immunity Litigation
A Guide for International Lawyers and Government Counsel
Newark: Sirius-C Media Galaxy LLC, 2010

Published by Sirius-C Media Galaxy LLC, 2010

Evidence and Burden of Proof under the Foreign Sovereign
Immunities Act, 1976
A Practical Guide for Business Lawyers and Government
Newark: Sirius-C Media Galaxy LLC, 2010

Sovereign Immunity Litigation in the United States and Canada
A Lawyer's Manual on Evidence and Burden of Proof
for Every Phase of the Trial
Newark: Sirius-C Media Galaxy LLC, 2010

Weber

The Foreign Sovereign Immunities Act of 1976:
Its Origin, Meaning and Effect
3 YALE STUD.WORLD PUB.ORD. 1 (1976)

Weiss, André

Compétence ou incompétence des tribunaux à l'égard des états étrangers
1 RCADI (1923) 525

West's Encyclopedia of American Law

Second Edition
New York: Gale Group, 2008

Wharton

Wharton's Criminal Law
14th ed. by Charles E. Torcia
Vol. II, §§99-282
Rochester, New York: The Lawyers Cooperative
Publishing Co., 1979

White, Robin C. A.

The State Immunity Act 1978
42 MODERN L.REV. 72-79 (1979)

Whiteman

Digest of International Law
Vol. 6
Washington, D.C.: Department of State Publication 8350, 1968

Wigmore, John Henry

A Treatise on the Anglo-American System of Evidence in Trials at Common Law
10 Volumes, Vol. 9 'Evidence in Trials at Common Law'
Rev. by James H. Chadburn
Boston, Toronto: Little, Brown & Company, 1981

Woodroffe & Amer Ali

Law of Evidence
14th Edition
Ed. and rev. by B. R. P. Singhal and Narayan Das
Allahabad: Law Book Company Ltd., 1979

Words and Phrases Legally Defined

Ed. by John B. Saunders
2nd Edition
London: Butterworths, 1969

Wright, Miller & Cooper

Federal Practice and Procedure, 1975

Y

Yaffe, Robert H.

Direct Financial Effects under the Foreign Sovereign Immunities Act
14 LAW.AMERICAS 361-365 (1982)

Yannopoulos, A. N.

*Foreign sovereign immunity and the arrest of state-owned ships:
the need for an admiralty foreign sovereign immunities act*
57 TUL.L.REV. 1274-1342 (1983)

FROM THE SAME AUTHOR

A Bibliography

ISBNs shall not be referenced for the reason that I publish with different outlets and publishers, using various ISBN blocks. The ISBN numbers, if needed, can be found on ipublica.com. They are always referenced with the publication.

You can search publications from here:
http://ipublica.com/books/

For audio books and music, you can start here:
http://ipublica.com/audio/

All paperbacks, audio downloads, audio book compact discs, music downloads and music compact discs, as well as Kindle books, are referenced on the site.

For free podcasts search iTunes under my author name.

For quoting my publications, please use the following form:
Pierre F. Walter, [Title]: [Subtitle], Newark: Sirius-C Media Galaxy LLC, 2010

English Publications

by Pierre F. Walter

Awareness Guides

The Idiot Guide to Consciousness
Newark: Sirius-C Media Galaxy LLC, 2010

The Idiot Guide to Creativity and Career
Newark: Sirius-C Media Galaxy LLC, 2010

The Idiot Guide to Emotions
Newark: Sirius-C Media Galaxy LLC, 2010

The Idiot Guide to Intuition
Newark: Sirius-C Media Galaxy LLC, 2010

The Idiot Guide to Love
Newark: Sirius-C Media Galaxy LLC, 2010

The Idiot Guide to Sanity
Newark: Sirius-C Media Galaxy LLC, 2010

The Idiot Guide to Science
Newark: Sirius-C Media Galaxy LLC, 2010

The Idiot Guide to Servant Leadership
Newark: Sirius-C Media Galaxy LLC, 2010

The Idiot Guide to Soul Power
Newark: Sirius-C Media Galaxy LLC, 2010

The Idiot Guide to World Peace
Newark: Sirius-C Media Galaxy LLC, 2010

Audio Books

A Psychological Revolution?
On the Teaching of Krishnamurti
Newark: Sirius-C Media Galaxy LLC, 2010

Child Play
Coaching Your Inner Child
Newark: Sirius-C Media Galaxy LLC, 2010

Consciousness and Shamanism
An Ayahuasca Experience
Newark: Sirius-C Media Galaxy LLC, 2010

Creative Prayer
The Miracle Road
Newark: Sirius-C Media Galaxy LLC, 2010

Eight Dynamic Patterns of Living
Base Elements of True Civilization
Newark: Sirius-C Media Galaxy LLC, 2010

Emonics
A Systemic Analysis of Emotional Identity in the Etiology of Sexual
Paraphilias
Newark: Sirius-C Media Galaxy LLC, 2010

Emotional Flow
A Holistic Approach to Healing Sadism
Newark: Sirius-C Media Galaxy LLC, 2010

Love and Morality
A Study of the Roots of Violence
Newark: Sirius-C Media Galaxy LLC, 2010

Love or Laws?
When Law Punishes Life
Newark: Sirius-C Media Galaxy LLC, 2010

Published by Sirius-C Media Galaxy LLC, 2010

Minotaur Unveiled
A Historical Assessment of Adult-Child Sexual Interaction
Newark: Sirius-C Media Galaxy LLC, 2010

Notes on Consciousness
Elements of an Integrative Worldview
Newark: Sirius-C Media Galaxy LLC, 2010

Oedipal Hero
The Hidden Side of Glory
Newark: Sirius-C Media Galaxy LLC, 2010

Orgonomy and Schizophrenia
An Unpublished Case Report by Wilhelm Reich
Newark: Sirius-C Media Galaxy LLC, 2010

Patterns of Perception
Preferred Pathways to Genius
Newark: Sirius-C Media Galaxy LLC, 2010

Power or Depression?
The Cultural Roots of Abuse
Newark: Sirius-C Media Galaxy LLC, 2010

Processed Reality
Pitfalls of Perception and the Cosmic Mind
Newark: Sirius-C Media Galaxy LLC, 2010

Reich's Greatest Discoveries
An Essay on Wilhelm Reich
Newark: Sirius-C Media Galaxy LLC, 2010

Sane Child vs. Insane Society
Some Thoughts on Education
Newark: Sirius-C Media Galaxy LLC, 2010

Soul Jazz
Recognizing and Realizing Your Soul Values
Newark: Sirius-C Media Galaxy LLC, 2010

The Aquarius Age

What the Zodiac Reveals About the New Age
Newark: Sirius-C Media Galaxy LLC, 2010

The Drug Trap

Some Ideas Regarding Substance Abuse
Newark: Sirius-C Media Galaxy LLC, 2010

The Hero Culture

Annotations on Insanity
Newark: Sirius-C Media Galaxy LLC, 2010

The I Ching's Perennial Pro-Life Code

An Analysis of Pattern
Newark: Sirius-C Media Galaxy LLC, 2010

The Legal Split in Child Protection

Overcoming the Double Standard
Newark: Sirius-C Media Galaxy LLC, 2010

The Lunar Bull

Spiritual Significance of Matriarchy
Newark: Sirius-C Media Galaxy LLC, 2010

The Star Script

Astrology and Personal Growth
Newark: Sirius-C Media Galaxy LLC, 2010

The Webolution

A Publishing Highway?
Newark: Sirius-C Media Galaxy LLC, 2010

Book and Media Reviews

---

110 Bestselling Books Reviewed by Pierre F. Walter

Newark: Sirius-C Media Galaxy LLC, 2010

Published by Sirius-C Media Galaxy LLC, 2010

Great Minds from Leonardo to Fritjof Capra
Newark: Sirius-C Media Galaxy LLC, 2010

Encyclopedias

Walter's Encyclopedia
Academic Edition
Newark: Sirius-C Media Galaxy LLC, 2010

Walter's Encyclopedia
Illustrated Edition
Newark: Sirius-C Media Galaxy LLC, 2010

Monographs

Do You Love Einstein?
Creative Insights On Perennial Wisdom, Human Genius and the
Quantum Field
Newark: Sirius-C Media Galaxy LLC, 2010

Energy Science and Vibrational Healing
A Systems Approach Human Emotions and Sexuality
Newark: Sirius-C Media Galaxy LLC, 2010

Evidence and Burden of Proof in
Foreign Sovereign Immunity Litigation
A Guide for International Lawyers and Government Counsel
Newark: Sirius-C Media Galaxy LLC, 2010

Evidence and Burden of Proof under the
Foreign Sovereign Immunities Act, 1976
A Practical Guide for Business Lawyers and Government
Newark: Sirius-C Media Galaxy LLC, 2010

Love and Awareness

A Consciousness for the New Age
Newark: Sirius-C Media Galaxy LLC, 2010

Love or Morality?

Social Policy for the 21st Century
Newark: Sirius-C Media Galaxy LLC, 2010

Natural Order

Thesis, Antithesis and Synthesis in Human Evolution
Newark: Sirius-C Media Galaxy LLC, 2010

Normative Psychoanalysis

How the Oedipal Dogma Shapes Consumer Culture
Newark: Sirius-C Media Galaxy LLC, 2010

Sovereign Immunity Litigation in the United States and Canada

A Lawyer's Manual on Evidence and Burden of Proof
for Every Phase of the Trial
Newark: Sirius-C Media Galaxy LLC, 2010

The Deeper Yielding

Commentaries on Loving
Newark: Sirius-C Media Galaxy LLC, 2010

The Life Authoring Manual

An Integrated Approach to Personal Growth
Newark: Sirius-C Media Galaxy LLC, 2010

The Restriction of National Sovereignty

From the Early Peace Plans to a World Government
Newark: Sirius-C Media Galaxy LLC, 2010

The Science of Orgonomy

A Study on Wilhelm Reich
Newark: Sirius-C Media Galaxy LLC, 2010

The Science of Shamanism

Millenary Model for an Integrative Worldview
Newark: Sirius-C Media Galaxy LLC, 2010

Published by Sirius-C Media Galaxy LLC, 2010

Poetic Writings and Audio Books

Poetic Writings

Stories, Pamphlets, Poetry, Changing the Love Pattern, The Hero Cult, The Trial
Newark: Sirius-C Media Galaxy LLC, 2010

Mona Lisa Pamphlets (Audio Book)

Paraculture, Alkibiades, Princess Love
Newark: Sirius-C Media Galaxy LLC, 2010

True Stories (Audio Book)

Short Stories of Six Children
Newark: Sirius-C Media Galaxy LLC, 2010

Yami (Audio Book)

Short Story in Twelve Parts
Newark: Sirius-C Media Galaxy LLC, 2010

Scholarly Articles

Alternative Medicine and Wellness Techniques

14 Pathways to Health
Newark: Sirius-C Media Galaxy LLC, 2010

Aquarius Age and Publishing

A New Paradigm Emerging
Newark: Sirius-C Media Galaxy LLC, 2010

Basics of Career Design

Opening Inner Space
Newark: Sirius-C Media Galaxy LLC, 2010

Basics of Divination

How Divination Can Facilitate Smart Decision-Making
Newark: Sirius-C Media Galaxy LLC, 2010

Basics of Feng Shui
An Old Energy Science
Newark: Sirius-C Media Galaxy LLC, 2010

Basics of Mythology
Some Leading Archetypes
Newark: Sirius-C Media Galaxy LLC, 2010

Basics of Potential Astrology
How Potential Astrology Can Help You Find the Work You Love
Newark: Sirius-C Media Galaxy LLC, 2010

Basics of the Science of Mind
The Twelve Branches of the Tree of Knowledge
Newark: Sirius-C Media Galaxy LLC, 2010

Krishnamurti, Vedanta and the Denial of Pleasure
A Philosopher Redefines Human Nature
Newark: Sirius-C Media Galaxy LLC, 2010

Permissive Education
A Summary
Newark: Sirius-C Media Galaxy LLC, 2010

Taoism and the I Ching
Understanding Nonaction and Right Action
Newark: Sirius-C Media Galaxy LLC, 2010

The Inner Journey
Awakening Your Inner Artist
Newark: Sirius-C Media Galaxy LLC, 2010

The Mythology of Narcissism
Pathology of the Consumer Age
Newark: Sirius-C Media Galaxy LLC, 2010

Published by Sirius-C Media Galaxy LLC, 2010

French Publications

by Pierre F. Walter

Essais

Essais 1990-2010
Newark: Sirius-C Media Galaxy LLC, 2010

Écrits poétiques

Écrits poétiques
Newark: Sirius-C Media Galaxy LLC, 2010

Journal trilingue
Newark: Sirius-C Media Galaxy LLC, 2010

Livres Audio

Anissia
Histoire vraie
Newark: Sirius-C Media Galaxy LLC, 2010

Le jardin infâme
Un regard sur l'âme et son corps
Newark: Sirius-C Media Galaxy LLC, 2010

Une éducation amoureuse

Un regard sur l'enfant au naturel
Newark: Sirius-C Media Galaxy LLC, 2010

Potentiel et créativité

Au sujet du développement de soi
Newark: Sirius-C Media Galaxy LLC, 2010

Relations sans fusion

Au sujet du développement de l'autonomie
Newark: Sirius-C Media Galaxy LLC, 2010

German Publications

---

by Pierre F. Walter

Audiobücher

Die Ödipale Kultur

Wege aus der Verstrickung
Newark: Sirius-C Media Galaxy LLC, 2010

Macht oder Ohnmacht

Erziehung zum Missbrauch
Newark: Sirius-C Media Galaxy LLC, 2010

Fusion und Individuation

Von der Fusion zum eigenen Selbst
Newark: Sirius-C Media Galaxy LLC, 2010

Kaleidoskop der Emotionen

Ein Leitfaden zur Selbstfühlung
Newark: Sirius-C Media Galaxy LLC, 2010

Published by Sirius-C Media Galaxy LLC, 2010

Wilhelm Reich und Orgonomie
Eine Einführung in Reichs Orgonforschung
Newark: Sirius-C Media Galaxy LLC, 2010

Monographien / Essays / Artikel

Essays 1990-2010
Zwanzig Jahre schriftstellerisches Engagement in den Bereichen
Bewusstsein, Friedensforschung, Musikologie, Orgonomie,
Kinderschutz, Gewaltverhütung und Persönlichkeitsentwicklung
Newark: Sirius-C Media Galaxy LLC, 2010

Mehr als Kindersex
Historische, Ethische, Ästhetische, Psychologische und Rechtliche
Aspekte der Kindliebe
Newark: Sirius-C Media Galaxy LLC, 2010

Nationale Unmündigkeit
Abschied von der Heroenkultur
Newark: Sirius-C Media Galaxy LLC, 2010

Was ist Channeling?
Literaturüberblick und Zitate
Newark: Sirius-C Media Galaxy LLC, 2010

Poetische Schriften

Aphorismen, Gedichte, Balladen, Märchen
Gereimtes und Ungereimtes
Newark: Sirius-C Media Galaxy LLC, 2010

Drehbücher
David und Jonathan / David H. oder die Liebe zur Fotografie
Das Verfahren / Kurzdrehbücher und Sketche
Newark: Sirius-C Media Galaxy LLC, 2010

Frühe Jahre

Autobiographie 1955-1985
Newark: Sirius-C Media Galaxy LLC, 2010

Kleine Texte

Gedanken, Notebook, Traktate
Newark: Sirius-C Media Galaxy LLC, 2010

Pamphlete und Übersetzungen

Newark: Sirius-C Media Galaxy LLC, 2010

Romane und Novelletten

Erfundenes und Gesungenes
Newark: Sirius-C Media Galaxy LLC, 2010

Traktate (Audio Buch)

Eine Sammlung von Gesängen
Newark: Sirius-C Media Galaxy LLC, 2010

Wahre Geschichten

Newark: Sirius-C Media Galaxy LLC, 2010

Textbücher Lebensberatung (Bewusstseinsführer)

Wege zur Selbstentfaltung

Newark: Sirius-C Media Galaxy LLC, 2010

Wege zum Weltfrieden

Newark: Sirius-C Media Galaxy LLC, 2010

Published by Sirius-C Media Galaxy LLC, 2010

Web Presence

Pierre F. Walter on the Web

Sites

http://authoryourlife.com

http://ipublica.com

http://ipublica.net

http://ipublica.org

http://ipublica.tv

Video Channels

http://youtube.com/user/ipublica

http://youtube.com/user/authoryourlife

http://vimeo.com/pierrefwalter/channels

http://ipublica.blip.tv/

http://authoryourlife.blip.tv/

http://emosexuality.blip.tv/

http://pierrefwalter.blip.tv/

SYNOPSIS

Monographs-Audio

DO YOU LOVE EINSTEIN?

Creative Insights on Perennial Wisdom, Human Genius
and the Quantum Field
Newark: Sirius-C Media Galaxy, 2010

Introduction

'Why I love Einstein'

Do You Love Einstein?
Overview

Chapter One

'Perennial Insights'

Minoan Civilization
The Egalitarian Society
The Roots of Violence
Pleasure and Intelligence
Pleasure and Touch
Pleasure and Violence
The Holistic Science Paradigm

▸ A Matter of Terminological Correctness
▸ Ancient Wisdom Traditions
▸ Goethe's Color Theory

The Twelve Branches of the Tree of Knowledge

▸ Science and Divination
▸ Science and Energy
▸ Science and Flow
▸ Science and Gestalt
▸ Science and Intent
▸ Science and Intuition
▸ Science and Knowledge

- Science and Pattern
- Science and Perception
- Science and Philosophy
- Science and Truth
- Science and Vibration

The True Religio

- Generalities
- The Inner Selves
- Inner Child
- Inner Adult
- Inner Parent
- Inner Dialogue
- Multidimensionality of the Psyche
- Function of the Ego
- Inner Child Recovery
- Inner Child Healing

Chapter Two

'Integrated Knowledge'

The Forbidden Tree
Emotions and Cognition

- Emotions are Intelligent
- Emotions are Functional
- Emotional Self-Awareness
- Emotional Balance
- Emotional Intelligence
- The Human Energy Field
- Emotions, Sexuality and the Human Energy Field
- The Emotional Identity Code

Chapter Three

'The Nature of Genius'

The Spontaneous Nature of Creation
What is Creativity?
Genius and Inner Knowledge

Published by Sirius-C Media Galaxy LLC, 2010

Chapter Four

'Genius and Geniuses'

Four-Quadrant Genius
The Genius of Leonardo
The Genius of Wilhelm Reich

▸ From the Hero to the Human
▸ The Genius Defined by His Work
▸ A Scientific Genius

The Genius of Albert Einstein
The Genius of Fritjof Capra
The Genius of Françoise Dolto
The Genius of Pablo Picasso
The Genius of Svjatoslav Richter

▸ Some Autobiographical Notes
▸ Genius Research Applied
▸ Multiple Talents, One Decision, One Career
▸ No Prodigal Son, and No Prodigy
▸ Some Details of Richter's Genius
    • 1/12 Innate and Intuitive Musical Perception
    • 2/12 Correctness of Taste
    • 3/12 Perception of Whole Patterns
    • 4/12 Musical Intelligence and Eclecticism
    • 5/12 Impeccable Sight-Reading Capability
    • 6/12 The Ability to Play Complex Scores While Transposing Them
    • 7/12 A Natural Sense for Rhythm
    • 8/12 Musical Memory
    • 9/12 Faculty of Concentration and Physical Endurance
    • 10/12 The Ability to be Undisturbed
    • 11/12 Physical Constitution and Size of Hands
    • 12/12 A Man of Drama

The Genius of Keith Jarrett

▸ General Remarks
▸ Jarrett and Inner Knowledge
▸ Jarrett's Shostakovich

Published by Sirius-C Media Galaxy LLC, 2010

ENERGY SCIENCE AND VIBRATIONAL HEALING

A Systems Approach to Human Emotions and Sexuality

Newark: Sirius-C Media Galaxy, 2010

Introduction

'What are Emotions?'

The Energy Nature of Emotions
Overview

Chapter One

'Science and Emotions'

Introduction
The Myopic View
What Emotions Really Are
How Emotions Become Pathological
What Modern Scientists Say
Emotions and Schizophrenia

Chapter Two

'Handling Emotional Flow'

Introduction
Emotions are Functional
What is Emotional Flow?

▶ 1) Change (Flow)
▶ 2) Tao (Intelligence)
▶ 3) Yin & Yang (Duality)
▶ 4) The Five Elements (Interactivity)
▶ 5) Harmony (Equilibrium)

The Kaleidoscope of Emotions

- Rage and Courage
- Mourning and Individuation
- Joy and Sorrow

Integrating Emotions

Emotional Flow, Audio Book, 2010

http://ipublica.com/audio/en/consciousness/emotional-flow/

Chapter Three

'Healing Sadism'

Introduction
What is Sadism?
The Two Faces of Sadism
The Sadism of Child Protection
The Sadism of Modern Science
Fake Heterosexuality
Oedipal Culture
The Cultural Child Sex Dogma
Rape vs. Loving Embrace
Addressing the Other Victim
A Possible New Social Policy

Chapter Four

'Emotions and Sexual Paraphilias'

Introduction
A New Regard on Sexual Paraphilias
The Energy Nature of Sexual Paraphilias

- Carl-Gustav Jung (1875-1961)
- Paracelsus (1493-1541)
- Swedenborg (1688-1772)
- Mesmer (1734-1815)
- Reichenbach (1788-1869)
- Reich (1897-1957)
- Lakhovsky (1869-1942)

Published by Sirius-C Media Galaxy LLC, 2010

▸ Burr (1889-1973)
▸ Summary

The Huna Knowledge
Sex as an Emonic Expression
How Paraphilic Desire Turns Demonic
Sexual Paraphilias and Erotic Intelligence

Emonics, Audio Book, 2010

http://ipublica.com/audio/en/consciousness/emonics/

Chapter Five

'Transforming the Demonic Affliction'

Introduction
Healing the Luminous Body
Paracelsus' Aura Healing
From Hermetics to Quantum Physics
Framework for Holistic Healing

Chapter Six

'Six Steps to Change Your Emotional Reality'

Introduction
Facing Emotional Reality
Triggering Self-Awareness
Practicing Acceptance
Realizing Your Love
Facing Your Now
Making a Value Decision
Taking Action
Affirming Your Identity

Chapter Seven

'Harnessing the Power of Emotional Identity'

Introduction
Regaining Wholeness
Allowing Emotions
Developing Emotional Awareness
Developing Self-Vision
Become Flexible and Permissive

Chapter Eight

'Fritjof Capra's Essential Contributions to Holistic Science'

Energy Science is Holistic
The Turning Point
The Pioneer
The Systems Thinker
The Pragmatist

Chapter Nine

'Toward a Unified Cosmic and Human Energy Field'

Introduction
A New Old Science
The Hado Concept
Insights of Vibrational Medicine
The Human Energy Field
Morphic Resonance and Cell Vibration

▸ George Lakhovsky and Cell Resonance
▸ Ervin Laszlo and the Akashic Field

The Coherence Model
The Zero-Point Field
The Holographic Model

▸ Part One - A Remarkable New View of Reality
▸ Part Two - Mind and Body
▸ Part Three - Space and Time

The Enigma of Energy

Published by Sirius-C Media Galaxy LLC, 2010

Postface

'The New Energy Science'

Bibliography
From the Same Author
Synopsis Monographs-Audio
Notes

EVIDENCE AND BURDEN OF PROOF IN SOVEREIGN IMMUNITY LITIGATION

A Guide for International Lawyers and Government Counsel

Newark: Sirius-C Media Galaxy, 2010

Acknowledgments

'Thanks to my Mentors'

Preface

'The Complexity of the Burden of Proof Issue'

A Novelty Topic
Seven Immunity Statutes
Methodology
Terminology

Introduction

'Restrictive Immunity and Burden of Proof'

Chapter One

'The Law of Evidence and the Burden of Proof'

Introduction
Terminology

- ▸ Jurisdiction and Competence
- ▸ Statute and Law
- ▸ Fact
- ▸ Burden of Proof

The Evidential Burden

- ▸ Introduction
- ▸ Notion and Function
- ▸ Standard of Proof
- ▸ Incidence

The Persuasive Burden

- ▸ Standard of Proof
- ▸ Notion and Function
- ▸ Incidence

Chapter Two

'The Restriction of Sovereign Immunity'

State Trading and Sovereignty
The Allocation of the Burden of Proof
Immunity from Jurisdiction
Immunity from Execution
The Signal Function of Restricted Sovereignty

Chapter Three

'The Foreign Sovereign Immunities Act 1976 (United States)'

Introduction
Importance of the Act
Construction of the Act
The House Report

Published by Sirius-C Media Galaxy LLC, 2010

‣ The Burden of Proof
‣ Corrective Case Law
‣ Evaluation

Procedural Questions

‣ Subject Matter Jurisdiction
‣ Personal Jurisdiction
  • Minimal Contacts
  • Service of Process
  • Default Judgment
‣ Foreign State and Agency or Instrumentality of a Foreign State
  • The Legal Status of Romanian Bank
  • The Legal Status of MASIN
  • Credibility of the Affidavit
  • Formal Requirements Regarding the Affidavit
‣ Conclusion

The Burden of Proof for Jurisdictional Immunity

‣ Rule-and-Exception Construction
‣ The House Report Evidence Rule

The Exceptions to Sovereign Immunity

‣ The Waiver Exception
  • General Considerations and Burden of Proof
  • Arbitration Clauses
  • International Treaties
  • Conclusion
‣ The Commercial Activity Exception
  • Clause 1
  • Clause 2
  • Clause 3
‣ The Expropriation in Violation of International Law Exception
  • Expropriation in Violation of International Law
  • The Minimal Contacts Requirements
  • Conclusion
‣ The Immovable Property Exception
‣ The Noncommercial Tort Exception
  • Minimal Contacts or Nexus
  • Causality
  • Scope of Employment
  • Exception

▸ Conclusion

The Core Areas of Sovereign Immunity

▸ Overview
▸ Foreign Affairs
▸ Interior Affairs
  - Police Actions
  - Actions for the Protection of Natural Resources
  - The Price Fixing Procedure
  - Standards of International Law
  - The Court of Appeals Judgment
▸ Budgetary Activity
▸ National Defense
▸ Conclusion
  - Foreign Affairs
  - Internal Affairs
  - Budgetary Activity
  - National Defense

The Burden of Proof for Immunity from Execution

▸ Types of Execution Measures
▸ The Allocation of the Burden of Proof

The Exceptions from Immunity from Execution

▸ The Waiver Exception
▸ Usibus Destinata
  - Relationship between §1609 and §1610
  - Relationship between §1610 and §1611
▸ Conclusion

Conclusion

▸ Immunity from Jurisdiction
▸ Immunity from Execution

Published by Sirius-C Media Galaxy LLC, 2010

Chapter Four

'The State Immunity Act 1978 (United Kingdom)'

The Importance of the State Immunity Act 1978
The Construction of the State Immunity Act 1978
The Burden of Proof for Immunity from Jurisdiction

▸ General Considerations
▸ The Rule-and-Exception Principle
▸ The Restrictive Immunity Doctrine
▸ Examination of the Precedents
▸ Examination of the Restrictive Immunity Doctrine
    • A New Restrictive Immunity Rule
    • It is a New Independent Rule
▸ Examination of I Congreso del Partido
▸ The Burden of Proof for Separate Entities of a Foreign State
▸ Conclusion

The Burden of Proof for Immunity from Execution

Conclusion

▸ Immunity from Jurisdiction
▸ Immunity from Execution

Chapter Five

'The State Immunity Act 1979 (Singapore)'

Introduction

▸ Generalities
▸ Application of British Case Law
▸ The Burden of Proof Situation
    • The Burden of Proof for Immunity from Jurisdiction
    • The Burden of Proof for Immunity from Execution

Chapter Six

'The State Immunity Ordinance 1981 (Pakistan)'

Historical Development

Published by Sirius-C Media Galaxy LLC, 2010

Summery Thesis

Postface

> 'The Unasked Question'

Legal Materials
Abbreviations
Bibliography
Statutes

> 'On Foreign Sovereign Immunities'

FSIA 1976 (USA)
STIA 1978 (UK)

Table of Precedents

Notes

EVIDENCE AND BURDEN OF PROOF UNDER THE FOREIGN SOVEREIGN IMMUNITIES ACT, 1976

A Practical Guide for Business Lawyers and Government

Newark: Sirius-C Media Galaxy, 2010

Introduction

> 'Litigating under the FSIA 1976'

Chapter One

> 'Evidence Brief'

Introduction
Jurisdiction and Competence

Fact
Burden of Proof
The Evidential Burden
The Persuasive Burden

Chapter Two

'Assessment of the Burden of Proof'

Chapter Three

'Some Intricate Procedural Questions'

Subject Matter Jurisdiction
Personal Jurisdiction

‣ Minimal Contacts
‣ Service of Process
‣ Default Judgment
‣ Foreign State and Agency and Instrumentality of a Foreign State
  - The Legal Status of Romanian Bank
  - The Legal Status of MASIN
  - Credibility of the Affidavit
  - Formal Requirements of the Affidavit
‣ Conclusion

Chapter Four

'Solving Evidence Problems under the FSIA'

Rule and Exception Construction
The House Report Evidence Rule

Chapter Five

'The Burden of Proof for Immunity Exceptions'

The Commercial Activity Exception (§1605(a)(2) FSIA)

‣ Clause One
‣ Clause Two
‣ Clause Three

Expropriation in Violation of International Law (§1605(a)(3) FSIA)

Published by Sirius-C Media Galaxy LLC, 2010

▸ Introduction
▸ Expropriation in Violation of International Law
▸ The Minimal Contacts Requirements
▸ Conclusion
▸ The Immovable Property Exception

The Noncommercial Tort Exception (§1605(a)(5) FSIA)

▸ Introduction
▸ Minimal Contacts or Nexus
▸ Causality
▸ Scope of Employment
▸ Exception
▸ Conclusion

Chapter Six

'The Core Areas of Sovereign Immunity'

Overview
Foreign Affairs
Interior Affairs

▸ Police Actions
▸ Actions for the Protection of Natural Resources
  • The OPEC Price Fixing Procedure
  • Standards of International Law
  • The Court of Appeals Judgment
▸ Budgetary Activity
▸ National Defense
▸ Conclusion
  • Foreign Affairs
  • Internal Affairs
  • Budgetary Activity
  • National Defense

Chapter Seven

'The Burden of Proof for Immunity from Execution'

Types of Execution Measures
The Allocation of the Burden of Proof
The Waiver Exception (§§1610(a)(1), 1610(b)(1), 1610(d))
Usibus Destinata (§§1610(a)(2), 1610(b)(2), 1611)

- ▸ Relationship between §1609 and §1610
- ▸ Relationship between §1610 and §1611
- ▸ Conclusion

Conclusion

'General Conclusion'

Immunity from Jurisdiction
Immunity from Execution

Abbreviations

Bibliography

Statutes

Table of Precedents

Notes

LOVE AND AWARENESS

A Consciousness for the New Age
Newark: Sirius-C Media Galaxy, 2010

Introduction

'What is Consciousness?'

What is Consciousness?
Patterns of Perception
Overview

Patterns of Perception, Audio Book, 2010

---

http://ipublica.com/audio/en/consciousness/patterns-of-perception/

Published by Sirius-C Media Galaxy LLC, 2010

Chapter One

'Krishnamurti's Concept of Consciousness'

Introduction
The Way of Fear
The Content of Consciousness
Split Consciousness
The Individual and Collective Unconscious
The Role of Emotions
Emptying Consciousness of its Content?
Points to Ponder

A Psychological Revolution?, Audio Book, 2010

http://ipublica.com/audio/en/consciousness/psychological-revolution/

Chapter Two

'Eight Dynamic Patterns of Living'

Introduction
Eight Dynamic Patterns of Living

‣ Autonomy
‣ Ecstasy
‣ Energy
‣ Language
‣ Love
‣ Pleasure
‣ Self-Regulation
‣ Touch

The Autonomy Pattern
The Ecstasy Pattern
The Energy Pattern
The Language Pattern
The Love Pattern

- Culture and Pleasure
- Pleasure-Denial and Violence
- Compulsory Sex Morality
- Anthropological Evidence
- Love Osmosis
- Love versus Morality
- Rebuilding Trust

The Pleasure Pattern
The Self-Regulation Pattern
The Touch Pattern
Points to Ponder

Eight Dynamic Patterns of Living, Audio Book, 2010

http://ipublica.com/audio/en/consciousness/eight-dynamic-patterns-of-living/

Chapter Three

'Consciousness and Shamanism'

Introduction
What is Ayahuasca?
An Ayahuasca Experience
Hypothesis
The Consciousness Theory

- ▸ 1) The Ayahuasca Preparation
- ▸ 2) The Lasting Trance
- ▸ 3) The Shamanic Treatments
- ▸ 4) Focus and Intent
- ▸ 5) The Strange Reception
- ▸ 6) The Hypnotic View
- ▸ 7) Hypnosis and Natural Healing
- ▸ 8) Medical Hypnosis

Summary
The Cognitive Experience

- ▸ Alien Noise and Pulsation
- ▸ The Five Depth Levels
- ▸ Calling Me in Touch

Published by Sirius-C Media Galaxy LLC, 2010

- ‣ Freeing from Conditioning
- ‣ Love, Life and Relationships

Literature Review
Points to Ponder

Consciousness and Shamanism, Audio Book, 2010

http://ipublica.com/audio/en/consciousness/consciousness-and-shamanism/

Chapter Four

'The Spiritual Laws of Matriarchy'

Introduction
The Lunar Bull
Historical Turn
Murder of the Goddess
The Murder Culture
The Spiritual Laws of Matriarchy
Bull and Serpent
Points to Ponder

The Lunar Bull, Audio Book, 2010

http://ipublica.com/audio/en/consciousness/the-lunar-bull/

Chapter Five

'Processed Reality'

Introduction
Processing Reality
Pitfalls of Perception

- ‣ The Memory Matrix
- ‣ Processed Reality
- ‣ Self-Fulfilling Prophecies
- ‣ Unconscious Repetition Urges

Spiritual Pitfalls

- Churches
- Sects
- Gurus
- Saviors

Ideological Pitfalls
Emotional Pitfalls
The Myths of Worldwide Democracy

- The Myth of Child Protection
- The Myth of Civilization
- The Myth of Control
- The Myth of Culture
- The Myth of Education
- The Myth of Morality
- The Myth of Normalcy
- The Myth of Poverty
- The Myths of Religion
- The Myth of Science

Creating Reality
Points to Ponder

Processed Reality, Audio Book, 2010

http://ipublica.com/audio/en/consciousness/processed-reality/

Chapter Six

'A New Consciousness'

On Consciousness
On Love
On Power
On Science
On Health
On Emotions
On Peace
Points to Ponder

Published by Sirius-C Media Galaxy LLC, 2010

Notes on Consciousness, Audio Book, 2010

http://ipublica.com/audio/en/consciousness/notes-on-consciousness/

Bibliography
From the Same Author
Synopsis Monographs-Audio
Notes

LOVE OR MORALITY?

Social Policy for the 21st Century

Newark: Sirius-C Media Galaxy, 2010

Introduction

'The Tao of Love'

What is Love?
Love or Abuse?
Overview

Chapter One

'Toward a Functional Understanding of Love'

Introduction
The Cultural Confusion
The Cultural Fear of Erotic Novelty

Chapter Two

'On the True Nature of Human Sexuality'

Introduction
The Silent Taboo
The Myth of Pedophile Predator Sexuality

Chapter Three

'The Abuse-Centered Culture'

Introduction
Understanding Abuse as Accidented Love
Abuse is Cultural, Not Biological

Chapter Four

'The Demonization of Adult-Child Erotic Love'

Introduction
What is Child Protection?
Consumer Protection?
From Protecting Children to Serving Children
Sex Offender
Bibliography

Chapter Five

'The Commercial Exploitation of Abuse'

Introduction
The Institutionalized Victim
The Hidden Swine
Street Monster

- ▸ The Morality Smear
- ▸ Deprivation
- ▸ Depravation
- ▸ The Rationality Trap
- ▸ A Cover-Up Myth

Published by Sirius-C Media Galaxy LLC, 2010

Chapter Six

'The Patriarchal Love Bias'

Introduction
The Goddess Within
Emotional Abuse
Mind-Body Dilemma

Chapter Seven

'The Truncated Account of Adult-Child Erotic Attraction'

Introduction
Ancient Patriarchy

- The Sumerian Tablets
- Child Marriage
- The Relativity of Morality
- The Roman Games
- Child Prostitution
- Boylove and Pederasty
- Phallic Aggression
- Conclusion

Christianity

- Church-Ordained Child Murder
- Child Protection?
- The Demonization of Intergenerational Love
- Conclusion

Victorian Era

- The Virgin Cult
- Child Prostitution

Modern Times

- The Sadism of Protection
- Not Sex, But Violence Causes Trauma
- Not Just Freaks Love Children Erotically
- Erotic Feelings for Children are Universal
- Child Pornography
- Physical Child Abuse

Conclusion
Points to Ponder

Minotaur Unveiled, Audio Book, 2010

http://ipublica.com/audio/en/consciousness/minotaur-unveiled/

Chapter Eight

'Does Pedophile Love Equal Abuse?'

Introduction
Child-Adult Sex vs. Child-Child Sex
Possible Etiologies of Pedophilia
Possible Etiologies of Child Rape
Pedoemotions are Universal
Aesthetic and Poetic Childlove
Affectionate vs. Sadistic Childlove
Does Pedophilia Equal Child Rape?
Free Choice Relations for Children?
Lover vs. Offender

Chapter Nine

'Lovers or Abusers?'

Introduction
What are Sexual Paraphilias?
Is Childlove 'Sicko' Behavior?
An Etiology of Boylove
An Etiology of Girllove
Childlove vs. Perversion

Chapter Ten

'Love or Laws?'

Introduction
Childlove and Sensuality
Childlove and Normalcy

Published by Sirius-C Media Galaxy LLC, 2010

When Law Punishes Life
Statutory Rape
Child Molestation and Abuse
Law Reform
Love Reform

Chapter Eleven

'Free Choice Relations for Children?'

Introduction

▸ The Psychological Aspects
▸ The Legal Aspects
Sharing a Secret
Childlove and Incest
Overcoming the Split
The Great Sinner

Chapter Twelve

'The Roots of Violence'

Violence Begins Inside
Love and Morality
The Value of Permissiveness
Pleasure Defeats Violence
Breaking the Vicious Circle
The Tactile Imperative
The Birth of Functional Thinking
The Importance of Sensuality
Social Policy Considerations
Quest for a Distinction
For the Child's Best?
The Turndown of International Adoption
Child Play vs. Morality
The Love Continuum

Chapter Thirteen

'Child Protection Draft Bill'

§1 Preliminaries
§2 Competencies of Consultants
§3 Measures taken by Consultants
§4 Definitions
§5 Violence against Children
§6 Consent
§7 Degree of Violence and Burden of Proof
§8 Family and Educational Relations

Chapter Fourteen

'Handling Pedophile Desire'

Introduction
Accepting Your Childlove?
Coding Childlove
The Trap of Child Protection
The Trap of Morality

Chapter Fifteen

'A Policy Change Proposal'

A 12 Points Agenda

1. Crime Prevention is Longterm and Effective.
   Criminal Prosecution is Shortterm and Ineffective.
2. Possible Humans are the Rule. Impossible Citizens are the Exceptions from the Rule.
3. Public Sanity is Public Mental Hygiene.
   Republic Insanity is Absence of Governmental Hygiene.
4. Natural Intimacy is Conductive to Peace.
   Governmental Intimidation is Conducive to Civil War.
5. From Protecting Children to Serving Children. Free Choice Relations for Children.
6. More Public Education Makes for Less Crime. More Prison Miles Make for More Crime.
7. Free Education Serves the Child.
   Funded Disinformation Serves State Control Over the Child.
8. Politically Neutral Science Promotes Truth. Politically Correct Science Promotes Halftruths.
9. Humanism and Realism is Objective Perception.
   Idealism and Ideology is Distorted Perception.
10. Promoting Pleasure as a Positive Life Function Effectively Counters and Reduces Violence.
11. Homoerotic Affection gets Males into Balance.
    Homosexual Attraction gets Males out of Balance.
12. Promoting the Cause of the Sexual Child is not Pedophilia
    as the Cause of a Missed Childhood.

Published by Sirius-C Media Galaxy LLC, 2010

1/12 Crime Prevention, Not Criminal Prosecution

Crime Prevention is Longterm and Effective.
Criminal Prosecution is Shortterm and Ineffective.

- To Declare Harmless Behavior a Crime is Unconstitutional
- Nonviolent Sexual Behavior Removed from Criminal Regulation
- Mutually Consenting Sexual Behavior Handled by PEC Consultancy
- What is Pedoemotions Consultancy?
- Proposal 1/12

2/12 Possible Humans, Not Impossible Citizens

Possible Humans are the Rule.
Impossible Citizens are the Exception from the Rule.

- In the Aquarius Age Citizens are Customers, not Subjects to the Nation State
- Trusting the Goodness of the Citizen as a Rule for the Federal Government
- All Criminal Prosecution Without Primary Evidence is Unconstitutional
- Social Policy Making Done with Deliberate Focus Upon the Proactive Citizen
- Proposal 2/12

3/12 Public Sanity, not Republic Insanity

Public Sanity is Public Mental Hygiene.
Republic Insanity is Absence of Governmental Hygiene.

- Focus upon International, Global and Ecological Concerns,
  Not National Defense Paranoia
- The Leader Nation Leads by Example,
  Not by Doing the Contrary of What it Professes
- A Hero is Not a Mercenary Killer, Persecutor, Spy and Terminator,
  But a Full Human
- Proposal 3/12

4/12 Natural Intimacy, Not Governmental Intimidation

Natural Intimacy is Conducive to Peace.
Governmental Intimidation is Conducive to Civil War.

- All Sensual and Sexual Behavior is Prima Facie Part of Natural Behavior

‣ All Intimacy Enjoys Constitutional Protection
‣ Proposal 4/12

5/12 From Protecting Children to Serving Children

From Protecting Children to Serving Children.
Free Choice Relations for Children.

‣ Child Protection Equals Slaveholding and is Unconstitutional
‣ No Child Be taken from their Family on Hearsay and Without Primary Evidence
‣ No Child Be Labeled Sex Offender and Entered on Sex Offender Registries
‣ Children's Right for Body Pleasure is Protected by the Constitution
‣ No Criminal Punishment for Socially Adequate Behavior
‣ Proposal 5/12

6/12 More Public Education Instead of More Prison Miles

More Public Education Makes for Less Crime.
More Prison Miles Make for More Crime.

‣ A Simple Play of Numbers
‣ Nobody Can Think More in 24 Years than They can Think in 24 Hours
‣ Decades of Prison is a Hidden Death Sentence
‣ A Nation that Practices the Death Penalty is a Dead Republic
‣ Every Penny Spent on Defense and Less on Education Leads to More War
‣ Proposal 6/12

7/12 Free Education Instead of Funded Disinformation

Free Education Serves the Child.
Funded Disinformation Serves State Control Over the Child.

‣ Free Education Begins with Free Media.
  Free Media Means Non-Commercial(s) Media
‣ The New Media
‣ The Example Wikipedia
‣ How Free are Free Radios?
‣ Proposal 7/12

8/12 Politically Neutral Science, Not Politically Correct Science

Published by Sirius-C Media Galaxy LLC, 2010

Politically Neutral Science Promotes Truth.
Politically Correct Science Promotes Halftruths.

‣ More than 70% of American Scientists Are Funded by the Military.
  They are Not Neutral
‣ Science Requires Funding Also When Not Serving Defense Purposes
‣ Scientific Research Must Obey to Ethical Rules
‣ Scientific Research Should Not Require Peer Review
‣ Proposal 8/12

9/12 Humanism and Realism Instead of Idealism and Ideology

Humanism and Realism is Objective Perception.
Idealism and Ideology is Distorted Perception

‣ We Can Only Evolve from Where we Are, Not from Where We Wish to Be
‣ Realistic Social Policy Making Means to See the Human Positively,
  Not Ideologically
‣ Idealism and Ideologies are the Leading Paradigms Since 5000 Years.
  Where are We Now?
‣ Being Realistic in a Human World Means to Be Humanistic,
  That is, Human-Friendly
‣ Proposal 9/12

10/12 More Pleasure as a Positive Life Function Instead of More Violence as a Negative Pleasure Function

Promoting Pleasure as a Positive Life Function
Effectively Counters and Reduces Violence.

‣ As Pleasure and Violence are Mutually Exclusive,
  Society Must Foster Affectional Pleasure
‣ Social Policy Making Based Upon the Negative Human
  Brings Public Hysteria and Chaos
‣ The Human is Positive by Nature.
  It Becomes Negative in the Wrong Form of Culture
‣ Social Policies that Foster True Culture are Sensory-Positive
‣ and Build Basic Trust
‣ Proposal 10/12

11/12 Male Affection, Not Homosexual Attraction

Homoerotic Affection Gets Males into Balance.
Homosexual Attractions Gets Males out of Balance.

▸ Proposal 11/12

12/12 Promoting the Sexual Child is Not Pedophilia
Promoting the Cause of the Sexual Child is Not Pedophilia

▸ Proposal 12/12

Bibliography
From the Same Author
Synopsis Monographs-Audio
Notes

NATURAL ORDER

Thesis, Antithesis and Synthesis in Human Evolution
Newark: Sirius-C Media Galaxy, 2010

Introduction
The Child and Sanity
The Hairy Issues
Overview

Chapter One
Minoan Civilization
The Egalitarian Society
The Nonviolent Trobrianders
Yin-Yang Balance
Pleasure, the Prime Regulator

Published by Sirius-C Media Galaxy LLC, 2010

Oedipal Hero, Audio Book, 2010

http://ipublica.com/audio/en/consciousness/oedipal-hero/

Mysticism and Atheism

Published by Sirius-C Media Galaxy LLC, 2010

- ▸ Scientific Mysticism
- ▸ Mystical Thinking vs. Functional Thinking
- ▸ Mysticism vs. Spirituality
- ▸ Mysticism, Insanity, Cruelty, Brutality, Perversion and Fascism

Narcissism

- ▸ What is Narcissism?
- ▸ How to Identify Narcissism?
- ▸ Narcissism and Soul
- ▸ The Origin of Narcissism

Denial of Complexity

- ▸ The Etiology of Fascism
- ▸ Complexity and Simplicity
- ▸ Complexity and Consciousness
- ▸ Complexity and Child Abuse
- ▸ The Denial of Erotic Complexity
- ▸ The Denial of Children's Erotic Complexity

The Plague of Sadism

- ▸ The Etiology of Sadism
- ▸ The Abuse Pattern
- ▸ Sadism and Moralism

Conspiracy Thinking vs. Critical Thinking

- ▸ Generalities
- ▸ Dangers of Conspiracy Thinking
- ▸ The Biggest Secret
    - Pedophiles, Pedophilia
    - The Reptile Theory
    - The World is Being Dominated by Five Families
    - Blaming People or Institutions
    - Anti-Semitism
    - Secret Societies

Youth Fascism

- ▸ First Example
- ▸ Second Example
- ▸ Third Example

Chapter Three

The Eight Dynamic Patterns of Living

▸ General
▸ The Eight Patterns
  • The Autonomy Pattern
  • The Ecstasy Pattern
  • The Energy Pattern
  • The Language Pattern
  • The Love Pattern
  • The Pleasure Pattern
  • The Self-Regulation Pattern
  • The Touch Pattern

The Holistic Science Paradigm and Worldview

▸ A Matter of Terminological Correctness
▸ Ancient Wisdom Traditions
▸ Goethe's Color Theory

The Twelve Branches of the Tree of Knowledge

▸ Science and Divination
▸ Science and Energy
▸ Science and Flow
▸ Science and Gestalt
▸ Science and Intent
▸ Science and Intuition
▸ Science and Knowledge
▸ Science and Pattern
▸ Science and Perception
▸ Science and Philosophy
▸ Science and Truth
▸ Science and Vibration

The True Religio

▸ Generalities
▸ The Inner Selves
▸ Inner Child
▸ Inner Adult
▸ Inner Parent
▸ Inner Dialogue

Published by Sirius-C Media Galaxy LLC, 2010

Notes

NORMATIVE PSYCHOANALYSIS

How the Oedipal Dogma Shapes Consumer Culture
Newark: Sirius-C Media Galaxy, 2010

Chapter One

Introduction
Parent-Child Co-Dependence
Closeness vs. Clinging
What is Emotional Entanglement?
Emotional Abuse

▸ Emotional Entanglement Taken Serious
▸ The Primary Abuse Etiology

Chapter Two

What Means Oedipus Complex?
Is the Oedipus Complex Universal?
Criticism of the Theory

▸ 1/8 Restricted Validity
▸ 2/8 Cultural Conditioning toward Homosexuality
▸ 3/8 Distorted Psychosexual Base Structure
▸ 4/8 Mechanistic View of Sexuality
▸ 5/8 Nature Fosters Copulation, Not Masturbation
▸ 6/8 The 'Oedipal Family' Brings Perversion, Not Sanity
▸ 7/8 The Oedipal Theory is Pseudo-Science
▸ 8/8 Oedipal Reality means Cultural Slavery for Children

Oedipal Culture

▸ Castration or Permissiveness?
▸ Are Masturbating Children Better Citizens?

Published by Sirius-C Media Galaxy LLC, 2010

SOVEREIGN IMMUNITY LITIGATION IN THE UNITED STATES AND CANADA

A Lawyer's Manual on Evidence and Burden of Proof

for Every Phase of the Trial

Newark: Sirius-C Media Galaxy, 2010

Acknowledgments

'Thanks to my Mentors'

Preface

'The Complexity of the Burden of Proof Issue'

A Novelty Topic
Seven Immunity Statutes
Methodology
Terminology

Published by Sirius-C Media Galaxy LLC, 2010

Introduction

'Restrictive Immunity and Burden of Proof'

Chapter One

'The Law of Evidence and the Burden of Proof'

Introduction
Terminology

▸ Jurisdiction and Competence
▸ Statute and Law
▸ Fact
▸ Burden of Proof

The Evidential Burden

▸ Introduction
▸ Notion and Function
▸ Standard of Proof
▸ Incidence

The Persuasive Burden

▸ Standard of Proof
▸ Notion and Function
▸ Incidence

Chapter Two

'The Foreign Sovereign Immunities Act of 1976 (United States)'

Introduction
Importance of the Act
Construction of the Act
The House Report

▸ The Burden of Proof
▸ Corrective Case Law
▸ Evaluation

Procedural Questions

- Subject Matter Jurisdiction
- Personal Jurisdiction
  - Minimal Contacts
  - Service of Process
  - Default Judgment
- Foreign State and Agency or Instrumentality of a Foreign State
  - The Legal Status of Romanian Bank
  - The Legal Status of MASIN
  - Credibility of the Affidavit
  - Formal Requirements Regarding the Affidavit
- Conclusion

The Burden of Proof for Jurisdictional Immunity

- Rule-and-Exception Construction
- The House Report Evidence Rule

The Exceptions to Sovereign Immunity

- The Waiver Exception
  - General Considerations and Burden of Proof
  - Arbitration Clauses
  - International Treaties
  - Conclusion
- The Commercial Activity Exception
  - Clause 1
  - Clause 2
  - Clause 3
- The Expropriation in Violation of International Law Exception
  - Expropriation in Violation of International Law
  - The Minimal Contacts Requirements
  - Conclusion
- The Immovable Property Exception
- The Noncommercial Tort Exception
  - Minimal Contacts or Nexus
  - Causality
  - Scope of Employment
  - Exception
- Conclusion

The Core Areas of Sovereign Immunity

- Overview
- Foreign Affairs

Published by Sirius-C Media Galaxy LLC, 2010

The Burden of Proof for Immunity from Execution

The Exceptions from Immunity from Execution

Conclusion

Chapter Three

'The State Immunity Act 1982 (Canada)'

General Conclusion

General Conclusion

‣ The Burden of Proof for Immunity from Jurisdiction
‣ The Burden of Proof for Immunity from Execution
‣ The Means of Proof

Summery Thesis

Postface

Legal Materials

Abbreviations

Bibliography

Statutes

FSIA 1976 (United States)
STIA 1972 (Canada)

Table of Precedents

Notes

THE RESTRICTION OF NATIONAL SOVEREIGNTY

From the Early Peace Plans to a World Government
Newark: Sirius-C Media Galaxy, 2010

Introduction

'What is National Sovereignty?'

What is Sovereignty?
A Modern Definition
Overview

Published by Sirius-C Media Galaxy LLC, 2010

Chapter One

'The Rise of National Sovereignty'

The Necessity to Restrict National Sovereignty
Sovereignty Going Global?
The Empowered Citizen

- ▸ The Citizen Redefined
- ▸ The World Model Revisited
- ▸ Economolitics
- ▸ Growing Child Power
- ▸ A Changing Social Framework
- ▸ The Rights of Ethnic, Social and Sexual Minorities

Chapter Two

'The United States of Europe, Utopia or Future Reality'

Introduction
The Early Plans for Eternal Peace
Abbé de Saint-Pierre
Jean-Jacques Rousseau
Immanuel Kant
Saint-Simon
Coudenhove-Kalergi
Integration vs. Constitution

- ▸ The Integrational Model
- ▸ The Constitutional Model

A European Constitution?

Chapter Three

'The Restriction of National Sovereignty'

Introduction
State Trading and Sovereignty
The Allocation of the Burden of Proof
Immunity from Jurisdiction
Immunity from Execution
The Signal Function of Restricted Sovereignty

Bibliography
From the Same Author
Synopsis Monographs-Audio
Notes

THE SCIENCE OF SHAMANISM

Millenary Model for an Integrative Worldview
Newark: Sirius-C Media Galaxy, 2010

Introduction

'What is Shamanism?'

The Science of Shamanism
Overview

Chapter One

'What is Not Shamanism?'

Shamanism and Animism
Shamanism and Paganism
Shamanism and Parapsychology, Humanism, Theosophy

▸ Shamanism and Humanism
▸ Shamanism and Parapsychology
▸ Shamanism and Theosophy

Shamanism and Taoism
Shamanism and Zen
Shamanism's Model Function

Chapter Two

'The Warrior Scientist'

Published by Sirius-C Media Galaxy LLC, 2010

The Shaman's Roles
Shaman, Healer, Sage
My Shamanic Quest

- ▸ Prophetic Dreams and Spirit Visions
- ▸ The Turning Point
- ▸ Psychopomping Baginda
- ▸ Dreams Regarding Mother's Death
- ▸ The Sabdono Connection
- ▸ Renata
- ▸ Black Magic on Lombok Island
- ▸ Sujanto's Psychic Readings
  - Session One
  - Session Two
  - Session Three
  - Session Four
- ▸ Psychopomping Mother

Chapter Three

'The Shamanic Method'

Common Assumptions
The Detractors of Shamanism

- ▸ The Age of Enlightenment
- ▸ Cartesian Science
- ▸ Reductionism
- ▸ Catholicism

The Shamanic Revival

- ▸ Sigmund Freud
- ▸ Bronislaw Malinowski and Margaret Mead
- ▸ Carl-Gustav Jung
- ▸ The Grand Opening

The Shamanic Method
Science and Ecstasy

- ▸ Science and Divination
- ▸ Science and Gestalt

Chapter Four

'Shamanism and the Use of Entheogens'

Introduction
What is Ayahuasca?
An Ayahuasca Experience
Hypothesis
The Consciousness Theory

▸ 1) The Ayahuasca Preparation
▸ 2) The Lasting Trance
▸ 3) The Shamanic Treatments
▸ 4) Focus and Intent
▸ 5) The Strange Reception
▸ 6) The Hypnotic View
▸ 7) Hypnosis and Natural Healing
▸ 8) Medical Hypnosis
▸ Summary

The Cognitive Experience

▸ Alien Noise and Pulsation
▸ The Five Depth Levels
▸ Calling Me in Touch
▸ Freeing from Conditioning
▸ Love, Life and Relationships

Literature Review

Consciousness and Shamanism, Audio Book, 2010

http://ipublica.com/audio/en/consciousness/consciousness-and-shamanism/

Chapter Five

'A Science of Pattern'

Introduction

▸ 1) Autonomy
▸ 2) Ecstasy

Published by Sirius-C Media Galaxy LLC, 2010

Eight Dynamic Patterns of Living, Audio Book, 2010

http://ipublica.com/audio/en/consciousness/eight-dynamic-patterns-of-living/

Chapter Six

'The Matriarchal Science'

The Lunar Bull, Audio Book, 2010

http://ipublica.com/audio/en/consciousness/the-lunar-bull/

Chapter Seven

'A Scientific-Shamanic Approach to Religion'

Introduction
The Unique Self
The Secret and the Real
Body and Soul
Desire and Morality
Approaching the Divine?

Chapter Eight

The Integrative Function of Shamanism and Channeling

Introduction
On Consciousness
On Love
On Power
On Science
On Emotions
On Peace

Bibliography

From the Same Author

Synopsis Monographs-Audio

Notes

Published by Sirius-C Media Galaxy LLC, 2010

THE DEEPER YIELDING

Commentaries on Loving

Newark: Sirius-C Media Galaxy, 2010

Preface

'Love for Life'

Introduction

'What is Science?'

Book One

'The Deeper Yielding'

§01. A Quest for Truth
§02. The History of Childlove
§03. The Silent Software
§04. Reactions to Childlove

▸ A) Positively indifferent
▸ B) Negatively indifferent
▸ C) Positively subjective
▸ D) Negatively subjective
▸ E) Moralistic, judgmental, projective, defensive, pseudo-objective, negative, generalizing
▸ F) Positively affirmative, subjective, conscious

§05. The Abuse-Centered Culture
§06. Sex Offender
§07. The Fruits of Activism
§08. The Hidden Swine
§09. The Institutionalized Victim
§10. Mainstream Paranoia
§11. Mental Pornography
§12. Street Monster

Book Two

'The Deeper Meaning'

Book Three

'The Deeper Understanding'

Published by Sirius-C Media Galaxy LLC, 2010

THE LIFE AUTHORING MANUAL

An Integrated Approach to Personal Growth

Newark: Sirius-C Media Galaxy, 2010

Introduction

> 'A Comprehensive Technique'

Story Writing
Creative Prayer
Voice Dialogue and Spontaneous Art

Chapter One

> 'Author Your Life'

The Technique
The Personal Vision Statement (PVS)

▸ Global Vision
▸ Creative Realization
▸ Relations and Intimacy
▸ Fame and Merits

Your Global Vision
Creative Realization
Vision and Time
Relations and Intimacy
Fame and Merits
Revising Your Vision
Making a Wish List
Setting Your Goals
Points to Ponder

Chapter Two

'Creative Prayer'

Introduction
What is Prayer?
Learn the Technique
Practice Creative Prayer
Activate Self-Healing
Build Self-Confidence
Create Inner Peace

Creative Prayer, Audio Book, 2010

http://ipublica.com/audio/en/selfhelp/creative-prayer/

Chapter Three

'The Star Script'

Introduction
The Star Script

▸ Character and Talents
▸ Life Lessons
▸ Karmic Challenges
▸ Inner Maps
▸ The Intuitive Way

Your Life's Mission
Your Child's Vision
Your Moon Nodes
Your Soul's Desire
Realizing Your Strong Points

▸ Character and Talents
▸ Life Lessons
▸ Karma Lessons

Points to Ponder

Published by Sirius-C Media Galaxy LLC, 2010

The Star Script, Audio Book, 2010

http://ipublica.com/audio/en/selfhelp/the-star-script/

Chapter Four

'Healing Addiction'

A Common Etiology
Dealing with Addiction

▸ Why was I never addicted?
▸ Healing Addiction

Mind
Body
Emotions
Spirit
Dealing with Sadism

The Drug Trap, Audio Book, 2010

http://ipublica.com/audio/en/selfhelp/the-drug-trap/

▸ 1) Flow
▸ 2) Intelligence
▸ 3) Duality
▸ 4) Interactivity
▸ 5) Equilibrium

Dealing with Abuse
Acceptance
Realizing Your Love
Facing Your Now
Making a Value Decision
Taking Action
Affirming Your Identity

Chapter Five

'Building Your Inner Team'

Preface
Introduction
Prelude-Maternity
Who is Who Guide
Personal Diary
Creativity Central
Workbook

▸ Inner Child Recovery
▸ Inner Child Healing

Art Guide

Child Play, Audio Book, 2010

http://ipublica.com/audio/en/selfhelp/child-play/

Bibliography
From the Same Author
Synopsis Monographs-Audio
Notes

Published by Sirius-C Media Galaxy LLC, 2010

THE SCIENCE OF ORGONOMY

A Study on Wilhelm Reich

Newark: Sirius-C Media Galaxy, 2010

Introduction

'Queers and Quacks?'

Acknowledgments
Real Scientists
The Promethean Role of the Scientist
A Pioneer of Holistic Science
Overview

Chapter One

'The Genius of Wilhelm Reich'

From the Hero to the Human
The Genius Defined by His Work
A Scientific Genius

Chapter Two

'Reich's Greatest Discoveries'

The Nature of Orgone
The Einstein Affair
Reich's Pioneering Work

▸ References
▸ Essential Discoveries
▸ Defamed Yet Corroborated
▸ A Scientific Genius
▸ The Root Cause of Violence
▸ Advocacy for Child Sexual Rights

Implications

Reich's Greatest Discoveries, Audio Book, 2010

http://ipublica.com/audio/en/consciousness/reichs-greatest-discoveries/

Chapter Three

'Orgonomy and Schizophrenia'

Introduction
The Energy Code
The Schizophrenic Split

Orgonomy and Schizophrenia, Audio Book, 2010

http://ipublica.com/audio/en/consciousness/orgonomy-and-schizophrenia/

Annex

'Wilhelm Reich und Orgonomie'

Danksagungen
Einleitung
Zur Natur der Orgonenergie
Reichs Pionierarbeit
Reichs Wichtigste Entdeckungen
Reichs Faschismusforschung
Nachwort

Wilhelm Reich und Orgonomie, Audio Buch, 2010

http://ipublica.com/audio/en/consciousness/oedipal-hero/

Published by Sirius-C Media Galaxy LLC, 2010

Bibliography
From the Same Author
Synopsis Monographs-Audio
Notes

THE SCIENCE OF SHAMANISM

Millenary Model for an Integrative Worldview

Newark: Sirius-C Media Galaxy, 2010

Published by Sirius-C Media Galaxy LLC, 2010

Chapter Four

'Shamanism and the Use of Entheogens'

Introduction
What is Ayahuasca?
An Ayahuasca Experience
Hypothesis
The Consciousness Theory

▸ 1) The Ayahuasca Preparation
▸ 2) The Lasting Trance
▸ 3) The Shamanic Treatments
▸ 4) Focus and Intent
▸ 5) The Strange Reception
▸ 6) The Hypnotic View
▸ 7) Hypnosis and Natural Healing
▸ 8) Medical Hypnosis
▸ Summary

The Cognitive Experience

▸ Alien Noise and Pulsation
▸ The Five Depth Levels
▸ Calling Me in Touch
▸ Freeing from Conditioning
▸ Love, Life and Relationships

Literature Review

Consciousness and Shamanism, Audio Book, 2010

http://ipublica.com/audio/en/consciousness/consciousness-and-shamanism/

Chapter Five

'A Science of Pattern'

Introduction

▸ 1) Autonomy

Eight Dynamic Patterns of Living, Audio Book, 2010

http://ipublica.com/audio/en/consciousness/eight-dynamic-patterns-of-living/

Chapter Six

'The Matriarchal Science'

Published by Sirius-C Media Galaxy LLC, 2010

The Lunar Bull, Audio Book, 2010

http://ipublica.com/audio/en/consciousness/the-lunar-bull/

Chapter Seven

'A Scientific-Shamanic Approach to Religion'

Introduction
The Unique Self
The Secret and the Real
Body and Soul
Desire and Morality
Approaching the Divine?

Le Jardin infâme, Livre Audio, 2010

http://ipublica.com/audio//fr/le-jardin-infame/

Chapter Eight

The Integrative Function of Shamanism and Channeling

Introduction
On Consciousness
On Love
On Power
On Science
On Emotions
On Peace

Notes on Consciousness, Audio Book, 2010

http://ipublica.com/audio/en/consciousness/notes-on-consciousness/

Bibliography
From the Same Author
Synopsis Monographs-Audio
Notes

Published by Sirius-C Media Galaxy LLC, 2010

Equations are more important to me, because politics is for the present, but an equation is something for eternity.

– ALBERT EINSTEIN

I know not with what weapons World War III will be fought, but World War IV will be fought with sticks and stones.

– ALBERT EINSTEIN

NOTES

Annotations

[1] See, in particular, Pierre F. Walter, *Natural Order: Thesis, Antithesis and Synthesis in Human Evolution, Monograph (2010)*.

[2] *The Schooner Exchange v. M'Faddon (1812)*, 11 U.S. [7 Cranch] 116, 135 (1812).

[3] Alvin Toffler, *The Third Wave (1984)*, p. 81. (Emphasis mine).

[4] Id., p. 83. (Emphasis mine).

[5] Id., p. 87.

[6] Alvin Toffler, *Powershift (1991)*, p. 10.

[7] Id. p. 11.

[8] See Pierre F. Walter, *The Idiot Guide to Sanity, Awareness Guide (2010)* and Françoise Dolto, *La Cause des Enfants (1985)*.

[9] International law experts notably unite in the opinion that the United States have violated fundamental principles of international law by their invasion in Iraq, and this not only because they disregarded to comply with the advice and measures of the United Nations' Security Council, but for more general reasons. And here we are only talking about the invasion as such and not about the nowadays much more discussed fact that the US occupation powers systematically violate human rights on an almost daily basis by harassing the Iraqi population and mistreating prisoners of war, denying fundamental civil rights and fair trial to them.

[10] See the summery in: Claude-Henri de Saint-Simon & Auguste Thierry, *De la réorganisation de la société européenne (1814)*, Livre Premier, Chap. II, III in the edition of the *Centre de Recherches Européennes*, Lausanne 1967, pages 36, 37.

[11] Id., p. 37 (Translation mine).

[12] Jean-Jacques Rousseau, *Oeuvres complètes*, Vol. 2, Paris: Seuil, 1971, 333-352. Literally translated *'Excerpt of the Eternal Peace Project of Mr. Abbé de Saint-Pierre'*.

[13] Id., p. 347. In his novel *Émile*, Rousseau bites even more heavily referring to the famous priest as somebody with 'great projects and little insights'.

[14] Id., p. 334.

[15] Id., p. 335.

[16] Id., p. 340.

[17] Id., p. 347.

[18] Id., p. 341.

[19] Id., pp. 348. ff.

[20] *Kants Werke, Band VIII, Abhandlungen nach 1781 (1923),* 341-386. Literally 'For Eternal Peace'.

[21] Id., p. 349.

[22] Id., p. 354.

[23] Claude-Henri de Saint-Simon, *De la réorganisation de la société européenne (1967),* Livre Premier, Chap. II, III. The rather long title of the proposal was 'De la Réorganisation de la Société Européenne ou de la Nécessité et des Moyens de Rassembler les Peuples de l'Europe en un seul Corps Politique en Conservant a Chacun son Indépendance Nationale, de Claude Henri de Saint-Simon et son élève Auguste-Thierry (1814)'.

[24] Id., p. 27.

[25] Id., p. 35.

[26] Id.

[27] Id., p. 39 (Translation mine).

[28] Richard N. Coudenhove-Kalergi, *Paneuropa (1926),* Chapter XI, 1, p. 140. 'Pan' connotes 'all', 'entire' or 'whole'.

[29] Id., pp. 140-142 (Translation mine).

[30] See, for example, Pipkorn in Beutler/Bieber/Pipkorn/Streil, *Die Europäische Gemeinschaft (1982),* 1.2.2, p. 30. See more generally, Walter Lipgens, *Europa-Föderationspläne der Widerstandsbewegungen 1940-1945 (1968).*

Published by Sirius-C Media Galaxy LLC, 2010

[31] After the draft elaborated by Jean Monnet and Robert Schuman, the Montan contract was signed in a summit of the six founding members of the European Community on April 18, 1951 in Paris.

[32] See Art. 2 and Art. 3 EEC Charta where some 'tasks of the community' are enumerated, without however this description being final and definitive. The general opinion of European law experts here is namely that this clause is *soft* and that new tasks can be subsumed here as far as they do not contradict the general founding principles of the community and serve the day-to-day running of the community and the realization of its goals.

[33] Art. 105 EEC Charta only speaks of the 'coordination of the national economic policies'. The political union can thus not be realized under the present conceptual framework of the EEC Charta but needs a fundamental new agreement of all members of the EEC so as to enlarge the competences of the European executive forces and grant them direct executive powers within the territorial sovereignty of each member state.

[34] Bulletin of the European Community (Bull. EC), Addendum 1/1976.

[35] Paragraph I. B. 1, p. 13 of the Tindemans Memo.

[36] Paragraph I. B. 6, p. 13 of the Tindemans Memo.

[37] Bull. EP Nr. 50/1981, p. 31 und EA 1982/2, pp. 50 ff. See also the comment of Pauline Neville-Jones, *The Genscher/Colombo Proposals on European Union*, in: *Common Marked Law Review, Vol. 20 (1983)*, pp. 657-699.

[38] See Neville-Jones, id., p. 660 who writes: 'This was destined to be the single most contentious issue which more than anything else held up adoption of the Act by a full year'.

[39] See Eric Stein, *The European Community in 1983: A less Perfect Union?*, Common Marked Law Review, Vol. 20 (1983), pp. 641-656, 651-652; *European Political Cooperation (EPC) as a Component of the European Foreign Affairs System*, ZaöRV Vol. 42 (1983), pp. 49 ff.

[40] See EA 1982/2, pp. 45 ff.

[41] See Eric Stein, *The European Community in 1983 (1983)*, p. 651: 'E.P.C. is not a part of the community system, but it is closely linked to it through what one might call, a 'personal union'. The E.P.C. has no normative foundation.'

[42] Paragraph I. B. 1, p. 13 of the Tindemans Memo.

[43] See EA 1984, pp. 209 ff.

[44] See Werner Meng in: Groeben/Boeckh/Thiesing/Ehlermann, *Kommentar zum EWG-Vertrag (1983)*, §237, 23.

[45] EA 1984, pp. 209 ff.

[46] See Meinhard Hilf, *Die rechtliche Bedeutung des Verfassungsprinzips der parlamentarischen Demokratie für den europäischen Integrationsprozess*, EuR 1984, p. 9 ff.

[47] Gert Nicolaysen, *Vom Beruf zur Verfassunggebung in Europa - Fragestellungen zu einem Thema, EuR 1984*, pp. 94-97, at 96. (Translation mine)

[48] *The Schooner Exchange v. M'Faddon (1812)*, 11 U.S. [7 Cranch] 116, 135 (1812).

[49] See Pierre F. Walter, *Evidence and Burden of Proof in Foreign Sovereign Immunity Litigation, Monograph (2010)*, originally published as *Les problèmes de preuve en matière d'immunité de juridiction et d'exécution des états étrangers*, Genève: Université de Genève (Faculté de Droit), 1987. The study was recently published with amazon.com, both as a paperback and a Kindle edition.

[50] *Cross on Evidence (1979)*, p. 87.

[51] Public Law 94-583 (H.R. 11315), 90 STAT 2891-2898, 28 U.S.C. 1330, 1391, 1602-1611, 71 AJIL 595 (1977), 15 ILM 1388 (1976).

[52] The reason is that the FSIA links sovereign immunity to the subject matter jurisdiction of the court by the very wording of 28 U.S.C. §1330(a).

[53] Adopted by the General Assembly of the United Nations on 2 December 2004. Not yet in force. See General Assembly resolution 59/38, annex, Official Records of the General Assembly, Fifty-ninth Session, Supplement No. 49 (A/59/49).

[54] The affidavit is the usual means of proof in all foreign sovereign immunity actions. Not only can the foreign state prove its *prima facie case* with an affidavit, but also the plaintiff can put forward affidavits and documents in support of its motion, *Mol, Inc. v. People's Republic of Bangladesh*, 572, F.Supp. 79, 82 (D.Or. 1983).

Published by Sirius-C Media Galaxy LLC, 2010